BOBBY FLAY'S BARBECUE ADDICTION

BOBBY FLAY'S BARBECUE ADDICTION

BOBBY FLAY WITH

STEPHANIE BANYAS AND SALLY JACKSON

PHOTOGRAPHS BY QUENTIN BACON

CLARKSON POTTER PUBLISHERS
NEW YORK

Copyright © 2013 by Boy Meets Grill, Inc.
Photography copyright © 2013 by Quentin Bacon

All rights reserved.
Published in the United States by Clarkson Potter/Publishers,
an imprint of the Crown Publishing Group, a division of
Random House, Inc., New York.
www.crownpublishing.com
www.clarksonpotter.com

CLARKSON POTTER is a trademark and POTTER with colophon
is a registered trademark of Random House, Inc.

FOOD NETWORK and associated logos are trademarks of
Television Food Network, G. P., and are used under license.

Library of Congress Cataloging-in-Publication Data
Flay, Bobby.
    Bobby Flay's barbecue addiction/Bobby Flay with Stephanie Banyas
and Sally Jackson.—First edition.
        Pages   cm
    Includes index.
    1. Barbecuing. I. Banyas, Stephanie. II. Jackson, Sally. III. Title.
IV. Title: Barbecue addiction.
    TX840.B3F5194 2013
    641.7'6—dc23   2012034618

ISBN 978-0-307-46139-1
eISBN 978-0-7704-3346-8

Printed in Hong Kong

Book and jacket design by David J. High, highdzn.com
Jacket photography by Quentin Bacon

10 9 8 7 6 5 4 3 2

First Edition

TO MY DAUGHTER, SOPHIE

*Few things are more satisfying
to me than watching you
discover the foods and
ingredients that make you smile.
Love, Dad*

First and foremost, a big thank-you to my two co-writers and assistants, Stephanie Banyas and Sally Jackson, for their hard work and dedication to me each and every day. You both put 110 percent into every single project thrown your way. I couldn't do it without the two of you and, quite frankly, I wouldn't want to.

A special thank-you to the following people who also helped with this book:

Christine Sanchez	Kim Tyner
Renee Forsberg	Doris Cooper
Leia Gaccione	Pam Krauss
Peter Hansen	Chris Engelbrecht
Allene Arnold	Samantha Shuman
Justin Hunt	Jodi Burson
Kerry Miller	Jeanine Thompson
Dahlia Warner	Mandy Sheehan
Courtney Fuglein	Bullfrog & Baum
Quentin Bacon	Rock Shrimp Productions
Barb Fritz	Food Network
Marysarah Quinn	Kohl's
Ashley Phillips	Big Green Egg
Kate Tyler	Weber
Anna Mintz	Viking
Donna Passannante	Boos Board
Tricia Wygal	

My business partners, Laurence Kretchmer, Jerry Kretchmer, and Jeff Bliss

The staffs of Mesa Grill New York, Mesa Grill Las Vegas, Mesa Grill Bahamas, Bar Americain New York, Bar Americain Mohegan Sun, Bobby Flay Steak, and Bobby's Burger Palace

AND . . .

Rica Allannic, the best editor any author could ask for. Thank you for your continued support and friendship. You are quite simply the best!

CONTENTS

INTRODUCTION

THE WORD "ADDICTION" *almost always has a negative connotation. At the very least, it's associated with obsessive behavior. But in the case of my current addiction, my friends and family aren't planning an intervention. In fact, they encourage my obsession! And who wouldn't when it means the intoxicating scent of fruit woods wafting through the air and the neighborhood as smoke lightly kisses a pork shoulder for hours until it has turned the meat into a savory, achingly tender cut of sheer deliciousness?*

We all use the words "backyard barbecue" to describe an outdoor cookout. But true barbecuing means cooking food low and slow over an open flame. Most of the burgers and hot dogs served at your average backyard bash are actually grilled—meaning they're cooked quickly over a hot fire. Even though people often use the words interchangeably, or even generically, grilling is not barbecuing. I should know.

I love to cook outdoors, but until recently my main means of doing so was on a gas grill. As a New York City–born and –raised guy, I couldn't be bothered with all the fuss of tending to a charcoal fire and then having to clean up the mess. Well, I am older and wiser now and can appreciate the pros and cons of both gas and charcoal. And when I built my summer house in the Hamptons, I finally got the chance to try out everything. While I still love my gas grill, I have since opened my heart to other outdoor cookers: charcoal grills, smokers, pizza ovens . . . you name it. And while, yes, these are messier and more time consuming to cook on, they make food that tastes amazing.

As an American chef I have always looked to my native country for barbecue inspiration, and with good reason. We have a spectacular belt of states throughout the South to the Southwest that each has its own take on the most talked about cuisine in America. Even places such as the central coast of California and the Pacific Northwest have their own distinct style of outdoor, wood-fired cookery. Those dishes help define a cuisine that is distinctly American and are the topic of the greatest food debate in the fifty states: Which state has the best BBQ?

While I won't touch that one with a ten-foot pole, I can say that as time went by and my travels began to take me overseas, I realized that almost every country, every culture, has its own version of barbecue. Although I always thought of barbecue as an American pastime, grilling burgers and hot dogs with my family at the Jersey Shore (pre MTV) when I was four or five years old, it turns out we were just like every other place in the world that loved cooking outdoors.

Now I not only look to my homeland but across the world for flavors, techniques, and ingredients. In these pages you'll find Tuscan Rosemary-Smoked Whole Chicken (page 117), a tip of the hat to northern Italy, next to Smoked Ginger Chicken with Cardamom, Cloves, and Cinnamon (page 123), a distinctly Indian taste explosion. Slow-Smoked Pork Shoulder with Napa Slaw and Queso Fresco (page 152) shares these pages with Coconut-Marinated Pork Tenderloin with Green Onion–Peanut Relish (page 155). There are also recipes for quickly grilled dishes as well, such as Pimiento Cheese–Bacon Burgers (page 199) that has the American South written all over it, and Rib Eye with Goat Cheese and Meyer Lemon–Honey Mustard (page 189) that's straight from the center of Cali.

I get tons of questions while I'm standing in my restaurant kitchens, walking down the street, and of course more than ever on social media about grilling fish and vegetables. Most people think of those amazing aromas in our backyards as charred meats and poultry, but more and more, as we all try to be a little bit more healthful, fish, shellfish, and vegetables are finding their way to the grill and the smoker. One of the new staples in my house is

Hot-Smoked Salmon with Apples, Dried Cherries, Hazelnuts, and Greens (page 217) with an apple-cider-vinegar dressing for the crunchy salad; it's great for a crowd. Grilled Shrimp Skewers with Cilantro-Mint Chutney (page 256) make a great appetizer to get things started, along with Watermelon–Plata Tequila Cocktails (page 44). Be careful, they go down like lemonade!

You'll notice that the starters, salads, and sides chapter of this book is quite large. In my opinion, these dishes really help complete a table. So when you've got a serious barbecue going, make a handful of these: Fire-Roasted Corn with Mango-Habanero-Cilantro Butter (page 69), Grilled Eggplant Caponata Bruschetta with Ricotta Salata (page 77), Grilled New Potatoes with Queso Fresco and Grilled Green Rajas (page 95), Grilled Asparagus with Figs, Cabrales, and Sherry Vinegar Sauce (page 54).

I've also expanded my horizons when it comes to cookers. The majority of the sales in the United States these days is for gas grills, mostly because of the ease and consistency of the heat—plus, with their shiny stainless finishes, a lot of them look really cool in your backyard. However, a purist will use only live fire, and I have a few different grills these days. I love the Big Green Egg mostly for slow cooking and smoking. It has an amazing capacity for insulating the perfect amount of heat, and I find it to be super easy to use when it comes to smoking meats,

fish, and vegetables. I'll always have a classic Weber kettle around for quickly grilled ingredients that need just one chimney starter full of hot charcoal. One of my all-time favorite cookers is called a Caja China. I call it the magic box. It's terrific for things like a whole hog, whole pork shoulders, and whole turkeys for Thanksgiving. My new favorite grill is what I call a "crank grill," hand made by a gentleman named Chris Engelbrecht (see page 16). It makes life so easy because you can control the height of the grates for fast searing or slow cooking and you can escape those dastardly flare-ups. I love cooking chicken with the bone in and the skin on with this grill; it comes out perfectly crispy on the outside and juicy and flavorful all the way through because of the control. There are so many choices, but in these pages I go over the merits of many of my favorites so you have options if you are looking to acquire a new cooker.

As I am writing this, my mouth is seriously beginning to water. Time to get off this computer and over to my outdoor kitchen! I'm going to break out my chimney starter, fill it with hardwood charcoal (if you use lighter fluid you're fired from the grill), soak some wood chips, get out a spice rub, knock out a dipping sauce, toss together some slaw, and fire it up. If you can't tell, I'm addicted to barbecue. **NO INTERVENTION NECESSARY.**

IN MY MIND, *there are pros and cons to both gas and charcoal grills and smokers. Gas is quick and easy and clean, but doesn't add a lot of smoky flavor. Charcoal adds great smokiness but takes some patience and some skill. I love both and I use both, and almost all the recipes in this book can be made on any kind of grill. While you can pretty much turn any type of grill into a smoker (throw wood chips on charcoal or get a smoker box for a gas grill), if you're going to be doing a lot of smoking, or smoking meats for a long time, you may want to consider buying an actual smoker; I just can't recommend trying to use a gas grill to smoke meats for two hours or longer.* **I'VE LISTED** *some of my current favorite cookers here to help you in your search. But in the end, it's up to you to pick the grill that is right for you and right for your wallet. Whether you are looking for one that can smoke, grill up a storm, or just let you cook up a simple meal, there is something for everyone.*

CHOOSING A COOKER

GAS GRILLS

If you use a gas grill, all you need is a tank of propane gas or a natural gas line hooked up to your grill and you are ready to go for 95 percent of the recipes in this book—all except the ones that call for longtime smoking. You don't have to spend a fortune to get a good grill, but there are a few things to keep in mind when purchasing one.

Price: Gas grills range in price from around $300 to way more than $1,000. As with most things, you get what you pay for. So, for the most part, the pricier the grill, the better the grill. That's not to say there aren't some really great quality gas grills that don't break the bank, but you have to know what to look for.

Construction: Start by looking for grills made of stainless steel, my preferred material for professional cooking equipment—and also the most expensive. Keep in mind, though, that not all stainless steel is created equal. One thing to watch for is that not just the body is made of stainless steel but also the frame. There are many "stainless steel" grills that have painted steel frames that can rust. Once you decide on the material, look over the whole grill to see how it's put together. The biggest difference between expensive and inexpensive grills is the construction and heat distribution. Construction is extremely important for safety reasons. Heat distribution is important for even cooking. Look for grills that have at least two or more separate burners (not just control knobs), which will allow great control of heat. This is key for the recipes in this book that call for indirect grilling (see page 23).

Fuel: The next thing to take into consideration is the fuel: propane or natural gas. Natural gas requires a gas line at the location of your grill. Many grills can be bought in either configuration, but you can't run a propane grill on natural gas or vice versa. Many lower priced grills do not have the natural gas option, although more and more grills do these days. Watch the price, though. Some natural gas conversion kits can cost up to $100. Of course, natural gas will cost you less in the long run and save you trips to the store to fill up your tank.

BTU (British Thermal Units) rating: This is a measurement of the amount of heat created by the burner. A grill with a higher BTU doesn't necessarily produce more heat. It is a factor of the heat created, the size of the grill, and how well the grill holds and distributes that heat. Don't buy a grill just because it has a high BTU number. Compare that number with the size and the shape of the grill. Smaller, more compact grills can produce higher cooking temperatures with lower BTUs. A general rule to follow is 100 BTUs per square inch of primary cooking space.

Size: Once you have these factors decided, you need to pick the size you want. Think about the kinds of foods you will want to cook on your grill and how many people you might want to cook for. If you're planning on a large turkey or being able to cook up forty hamburgers at a time, you'll want a larger grill. If you cook just a few steaks or chicken breasts once in a while, you'll probably want a smaller one. Also look at the space you have. Get a grill that will fit safely and conveniently. Remember: It's not the size of your grill but how you use it that's important.

Features: Do you want a side burner? How about multiple-level cooking surfaces, a rotisserie burner, lights, or any one of a dozen things that get added to a grill? Remember that a basic grill will do a lot, and most of the extras get very little use.

VIKING GRILL

I have owned a Viking gas grill for more than fifteen years. I have spent most of my summers grilling up steaks and burgers and fish and chicken on one. It is my gas grill of choice both on my shows and at home.

CHARCOAL

There are many types of charcoal grills—small hibachis, kamado grills (such as the Big Green Egg; see page 17), and kettles, which are arguably the most popular and the ones I am primarily talking about here. Charcoal grills, in general, are much less expensive than gas grills and lend a great smoky flavor to foods cooked on them, but they do require planning ahead and a little more skill. The same criteria that apply to gas grills apply when purchasing a charcoal one.

Price: Charcoal grills normally range in price from $100 to $500 and, as with anything else, you get what you pay for here, too. I have been using a Weber kettle grill for years at home and on my shows and, while it's at the upper end of the price range, it is an excellent piece of equipment that, with proper care, has lasted for years.

Construction: A good solid construction is just as important for charcoal grills at it is gas grills, maybe even more so because you are dealing with open fire and hot coals. Type 1 steel has superior strength and is corrosion resistant. You really don't need to go for any bells and whistles when looking for a charcoal grill, but there are a few things to look for that will make your life a little easier (and who doesn't want that?). Basic elements that you should look for are:
- A porcelain-enamel finish on the bowl and cover; this makes for a practically indestructible grill.
- A tight-fitting cover; this is absolutely necessary for cooking larger cuts of meat, which require indirect grilling (see page 23).
- Top and bottom vents, to allow for good air flow.
- Two thick grates: one for the coal to sit on and one to cook the food on.
- Hinged grill grates, so that you can add more charcoal easily.
- A damper, which allows you to sweep ashes into it, is nice, so that you aren't left having to scoop them out yourself.
  Some charcoal grills have an electric starter, but I prefer to use a chimney starter (see page 19) to heat the coals.

Size: Consider how much grilling you will be doing. Mostly weeknight burgers, steaks, and fish fillets for a few people? Or are we talking about inviting over extended family or even the whole block for an afternoon cookout on a regular basis? Small grills are convenient in that you have to heat up only a small amount of charcoal, but they can be frustrating if you are trying to feed a crowd and want a larger surface area on which to cook.

WEBER KETTLE

This classic charcoal grill has become almost synonymous with outdoor cooking and can do practically everything, including smoking on a limited basis. It features a heavy-gauge porcelain-enameled cover and bowl, rust-resistant aluminum legs, and bottom vents that dispatch ash into a pan beneath the bowl. The iconic shape is key: It distributes heat evenly, allowing the hot air to circulate around the food as it cooks while keeping in the smoky flavor from the charcoal and any added wood chips. The large grilling area provides plenty of space for direct and indirect grilling and smoking (see page 23). You can even get an optional rotisserie kit. This has been my charcoal grill of choice for years.

ENGELBRECHT 1000 SERIES STANDARD BRATEN GRILL

A steel rotary crank on this charcoal grill allows you to adjust the height of the cooking surface to bring the flames closer or have them fall away. Both free-standing units or built-in grill options are available. At about $2,500, it is one of the more expensive charcoal grills on the market, but worth every penny, in my opinion.

SMOKERS

Long before the advent of refrigerators and chemical preservatives, smoke was used to preserve food, particularly meat and fish. Today, smoking foods is an art unto itself. Not only does it add incredible flavor, but it also tenderizes some of the toughest cuts of meat into some of the most tender.

You can definitely use a charcoal grill as a smoker—and a smoker as a charcoal grill, for that matter (just follow the manufacturer's directions that come with the cooker). The main difference between a smoker and a charcoal grill is that a smoker keeps the fire away from the food. A smoker keeps the temperature low enough to cook meats at 200°F to 250°F. A grill is designed to cook hot and fast, though it can be set up to do both hot and fast (direct) and slow and low (indirect) cooking (see page 23). While a smoker box can be used in a gas grill to add a hit of smoky flavor, this trick is best reserved for relatively quick-cooking dishes. For anything that requires two or

more hours of smoking, gas grills don't fare well, in my opinion, and I don't recommend using them for authentic smoking. So if you do a lot of barbecuing—the low and slow—look into a true smoker.

Fuel: The first thing to consider when researching a smoker is what fuel the cooker uses. Charcoal and hardwood smokers normally produce a more traditional flavor than propane and electricity; they also tend to be the most inexpensive. As the smokers using charcoal and wood are the only ones that I have experience with, I am going to refer only to charcoal smokers in this book.

Size: Not all of us have a lot of room to store a giant smoker. So when looking for a smoker, read up on how many people the smoker will feed. Also find out what type of food that particular smoker is good for making. On *Barbecue Addiction,* I use the small Weber vertical water smoker and the Big Green Egg. Two smokers that are on the opposite sides of the spectrum in terms of size and price but both do an equally good job when it comes to smoking a brisket or whole chickens or ribs.

WEBER SMOKEY MOUNTAIN BULLET SMOKER

If you are not sure you want to do a lot of smoking—and don't want to invest a lot of money before you find out—then I recommend getting a small, inexpensive, vertical water smoker. These are the least expensive smokers you can buy and will let you know whether you want to invest more on a fancier one at a later date or not. You can make good barbecue in these smokers, and for many it may be the only smoker you ever need. Its cylindrical shape makes it

look roughly like a bullet, and hence the name. The Weber Smokey Mountain is one of the best-selling bullet smokers ever and one of the cheapest ways to get started smoking.

THE BIG GREEN EGG

My favorite smoker and possibly the best ever invented is, in my opinion, the Big Green Egg. The Egg is a unique cooker, with unmatched flexibility and capabilities that surpass all other conventional cookers combined. It is a smoker, a grill, and an oven all in one, and you can cook literally any food on it year-round, from appetizers to entrées to desserts. The grill offers great heat control so you can decide the temperature at which you want to be cooking. Derived from an ancient clay cooker called a kamado, the modern Big Green Egg has undergone many improvements since it was introduced in 1974. Especially significant is the replacement of the clay used in early models with durable space-age ceramics developed specifically for the cooker to make it virtually indestructible. Of course you are looking at a lot more money for one of these than for a regular grill or bullet smoker, but it is an investment that is worth the money if you intend to do a lot of outdoor cooking.

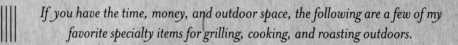

SPECIALTY COOKERS AND GRILLS

If you have the time, money, and outdoor space, the following are a few of my favorite specialty items for grilling, cooking, and roasting outdoors.

PARRILLA

This is a cast-iron grilling grate set over hot coals. Anything with a grate over direct heat can serve as a parrilla: a hibachi, a Weber charcoal kettle, or a Viking gas grill. The grate should always be about four inches above the coals. Begin the fire a good 30 minutes before cooking.

CHAPA OR PLANCHA

A flat piece of cast iron set over a fire, a chapa (which means "a piece of sheet metal") is good for quick cooking. You can also use a cast-iron skillet or griddle placed over the grates of a grill.

CAJA CHINA

Also known as a pig roasting box or a Cajun micro-wave, La Caja China is a wooden box lined with stainless steel that can cook a fifty-pound pig in about four hours—instead of eight—and a twenty-pound turkey in one and a half. It's a remarkable piece of equipment: You can even grill on top of the box (burgers, hot dogs, chicken skewers, etc.) while something is roasting inside of it.

ONCE YOU'VE GOT *your cooker, here are some essentials and tools that I recommend to make life easier when cooking outdoors.*

THE RIGHT STUFF

Chimney starter: This is the best and only way, in my opinion, to light a charcoal fire. Do not even *think* about lighter fluid; it is dangerous and makes your food taste like chemicals. Purchase the largest size chimney starter you can find (it should hold about 6 quarts of charcoal). Make sure the handles are sturdy and the construction is strong. These are inexpensive so you have no excuse not to get one. See page 23 for instructions on their use.

Charcoal: If you are cooking with charcoal, I recommend using natural hardwood lump charcoal, which burns hotter and cleaner than briquettes. The good news is that if you can't find natural hardwood in your area, you can order it online and have it delivered. If you opt for charcoal briquettes instead, stay away from those that are labeled self-lighting, which means they are saturated with lighter fluid—which contains petroleum. Trust me, you don't want to be ingesting those fumes or eating food cooked in them.

Grill baskets/toppers: I make my own grids for my Kohl's line, and I love using them for small items that will fall through the grates of the grill, such as asparagus, shrimps, mussels, and whole fish, whose delicate skin can stick to the grates of the grill.

Grill brushes: A heavy-duty grill brush for cleaning your grill grates is imperative; you will need it especially after grilling something with a sticky barbecue sauce or sweet glaze. Always try to clean the grates right after the food comes off the grill, when the grates are hot and the food hasn't had a chance to harden.

Tongs: A good pair of sturdy, stainless-steel kitchen tongs no longer than 16 inches is perfect for turning vegetables, chicken, ribs, and breads.

Spatulas: Heavy-duty stainless-steel ones are ideal for flipping burgers and fish.

Basting brushes: You can't have enough. I use them to apply oil, glazes, and sauces and prefer both silicone and boar's hair bristles.

Spray bottles: I like to have a bottle filled with water on hand to douse flames and flare-ups caused by grease dripping onto the heating element. Flare-ups can create an unpleasant char on food. I also like filling spray bottles with flavorful mops to spray on a brisket or pork shoulder when it is smoking.

Skewers, metal or wood: These are great for cooking shrimp quickly and for grouping smaller items that may fall through the grates, such as cherry tomatoes. Wooden skewers must be soaked in water for at least 15 minutes before putting them on the grill to prevent burning.

Thermometers, grill: If your grill or smoker doesn't have a built-in thermometer (usually in the cover) to monitor the temperature in the grill, I recommend that you invest in a grill surface one and set it on the grates of the grill to take some of the guesswork out of grilling, and especially smoking.

Thermometers, instant read: Instant-read thermometers are really important for the beginner griller/cook to help make sure food is cooked to the proper internal temperature; this is especially true when smoking, where you can't rely on as many visual cues to tell if food is done. To make sure the internal temperature is where it needs to be, use an instant-read thermometer stuck into the center of the food and avoid touching the bone.

Smoker box or foil pouches: If you own a gas grill and want to flavor your food with smoke, you can use one of these. Smoker boxes can be found in home stores and online. They are usually made of anything from cast iron to cheap metal; I recommend spending a little more and going with cast iron or stainless steel. Simply fill the box with drained, soaked wood chips; close the cover; and put the box on the grates of the grill. Or you can make a foil pouch: Wrap the drained, soaked wood chips in heavy-duty foil to make a secure packet, poke 8 to 10 holes into the top of the foil using a knife or skewer, and put on the grates of the grill. Close the cover and let the smoke build.

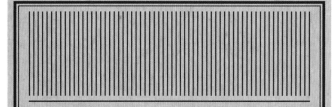

CLEANING THE GRATES

For obvious reasons, it is always important to start with a clean grill, and if you get into the habit of cleaning the grill immediately after you finish grilling, your life will become so much easier. (If you wait until the grilled-on food gets cold and hardens, it will become more difficult and time consuming to clean the next time you grill.) Use a heavy-duty grill brush (see page 20) and then use kitchen tongs (see page 20) to rub the grates with several folded heavy-duty paper towels that you've dipped in cooking oil. This will help get off the last remnants of food that the brush left behind and to create a nonstick surface for the next time you grill. It takes only a few minutes, and you can do it while your food is resting.

You've got your grill, you've got your gear. Now get outside and get cooking!

TENDING THE FIRE

START YOUR ENGINES

Regardless of which fuel you choose, you have to give your grill enough time to heat up. Think of it like preheating your oven. (In fact, if you think of your grill as an outdoor oven, it may take some of the pressure off and make grilling less intimidating.)

GAS GRILL

Make sure your propane tank is full or that you have a full spare tank. Nothing spoils an outdoor party faster than running out of fuel when your food is only halfway cooked. Start by turning all the burners to the highest settings 15 to 30 minutes before cooking and make sure the cover is closed. Every time you open the cover (just like every time you open the door of the oven), heat escapes. Also keep in mind that you are cooking outdoors, where it can be cooler than inside of your home, depending on the time of the year.
Direct grilling: If you are grilling something small that requires intense heat and quick cooking times, leave the burners on high.
Indirect grilling: If you will be grilling something larger that requires both direct and indirect grilling, turn some of the burners off so that you have direct heat. If you have a gas grill with two burners, turn one of the burners down to low. If you have a three-burner grill, keep the outside two on high and turn off the middle burner completely.

CHARCOAL GRILL

My method, in fact the *only* method, in my opinion, for starting a fire in a charcoal grill is to use a chimney starter (see page 19). Fill the chimney to the top with charcoal, stuff the bottom with newspaper, and set the chimney on the bottom grill grates. Light the paper and leave the whole setup alone until the coals are glowing and covered in white ash, 20 to 30 minutes. Carefully dump the coals into the grill and arrange them for direct or indirect grilling (see below). Then add the grilling grate, put on the cover, and let the cooking grate heat for at least 15 minutes before you add your food.
Direct grilling: Rake the coals into an even layer for quick, high-heat grilling.
Indirect grilling: Bank the hot coals in a pile on one side of the grill (or arrange them around the perimeter of the grill). This will allow you to grill directly over the hot coals or indirectly over the cooler area (not over the coals).

HOW HOT IS HOT?

Just as a chef's way to test the doneness of meat is by feel, the experienced barbecuer's way to test the heat of the fire is with the hand test. This method involves holding the outstretched palm of your hand an inch or two above the grill grate. The length of time you can hold it there will tell you approximately what the temperature is. However, if you want complete accuracy, use the grill's thermometer or an oven thermometer set on the grates of the grill.

Less than 1 second	very hot	around 600°F
2 seconds	hot	400°F to 500°F
4 seconds	medium	350°F to 375°F
6 seconds	medium-low	325°F to 350°F

LOW-AND-SLOW COOKING AND SMOKING

What kind of food needs to be cooked low and slow? Whole chickens, large roasts such as brisket and pork shoulders, whole turkeys, legs of lamb. The obvious reason for this method is so that the outside of the meat doesn't burn before the inside of the meat is cooked to the proper temperature. Make sure you are using a grill thermometer to monitor the temperature inside the grill.

Smoking is a process of cooking tough cuts of meats until tender and flavorful. The temperature is kept low so that the smoke has enough time to sink into the meat. The long cooking time also breaks down the connective fibers in the meat so that tough cuts of meat become really tender and sweet—just as braising does in a low oven. Smoking is really an art, not a science, and, like anything, it requires practice and some patience. It is best done in the range of 200°F to 225°F. For safety reasons, most meats need to be cooked to an internal temperature of 145°F and poultry to at least 160°F. But, to get the most tender brisket, ribs, or pulled pork, you will need to cook to a temperature of 180°F.

SMOKER

Set up your smoker according to the manufacturer's directions. Use a chimney starter to heat the coals (see page 19). You will need anywhere from 6 to 10 pounds of hot coals, depending on what you are cooking; the more charcoal you use, the longer the heat will last. Add the hot coals to the charcoal pan and add your drained, soaked wood chips now, too. Heat enough water to fill the enamel water pan about three-quarters full. (You want the water to be hot so that the coals don't have to heat it.) Put the water pan in the barrel (the tall part of the smoker) on the bottom hooks and add the hot water. Carefully put the barrel on the charcoal pan section. Replace the wire racks in the barrel, one on top of the water pan and the other on top of the hooks. Open the side vents all the way, let smoke build for 10 minutes, and then aim to keep the temperature at between 200°F and 250°F for most smoking recipes; use a grill thermometer to monitor the heat.

Keep the cover closed as much as you can once you've added your food to the smoker; every time you open the cover you let out smoke and heat. You can control the internal temperature of the smoker by opening or closing the side vents and adjusting the top vent or chimney. Opening the side vents fully will raise the temperature; closing them partially will tame the heat—and closing them completely will extinguish the fire. During long smoking periods, maintain the temperature by adding hot coals every hour. (You may want to add more wood chips, depending on your recipe and how smoky you want your food.) It's better to start slow and add a few coals than to have to try to lower the temperature once you've added too many. If that happens, just open the cover to decrease the temperature.

CHARCOAL GRILL

Set up your grill for indirect grilling (see page 23), arranging a drip pan (can be the disposable aluminum kind you find at supermarkets) next to the banked coals. For smoking, add drained, soaked wood chips to the coals. Open the vents on the top and bottom and position the lid so that the open vent is over the cooler side, opposite the heat. The vents will draw air through the fire, swirling smoke over the food before it leaves the grill. Once the grill is hot, fill the drip pan with a couple of inches of water. Adjust the vents to keep the temperature between 200°F and 250°F for smoking.

After a while, the coals will start to extinguish, and you'll need to replenish them to maintain the heat; use the chimney starter each time (set it on a heatproof surface) to get more coals good and hot before adding them to your grill. You are going to need to add about 15 hot coals to each pile of charcoal every hour or so. Keep in mind that it takes 20 to 30 minutes to light a full starter full of charcoal. Add additional soaked wood chips with each addition of new coal, or as desired.

TOP  10 TIPS FOR PERFECT BACKYARD BARBECUES

1. PREP IN ADVANCE

Don't wait until your friends arrive to start brining chicken, marinating lamb, or even forming burgers for that matter. Prepping in advance is key for any kind of party, outdoor ones included. Having most of the work done ahead of time frees you up to spend more time with your guests. Salads and relishes can be prepped a day ahead; veggies for the grill can be sliced; and pitchers of cocktails can be mixed in advance and refrigerated until guests arrive. Fill your chimney starter with charcoal and newspaper or have your gas grill preheating. Remember that preparation is half the battle.

2. GET ORGANIZED

Before you light that first coal or flip the switch on your gas grill, make sure you have everything you need nearby so that you don't have to run back and forth into your house to find that pair of tongs or peppermill while your food is burning on the grill.

3. HAVE EXTRA EVERYTHING

Make sure you have enough charcoal and wood chips; keep a spare gas tank on hand in case yours runs out in the middle of grilling dinner for ten of your closest friends. If someone wants to know what to bring, say a bag of ice! Which leads me to . . .

4. STOCK THE COOLER

You can make a signature cocktail or serve beer and wine—just make sure it's easy for guests to serve themselves and that everything is nice and cold when they arrive. Nobody likes warm beer, well except for the British . . .

5. HAVE SOMETHING READY TO NIBBLE ON

Whether you make a dip or cold appetizer that can be ready and waiting, or you've planned a super-quick grilled dish to start, make sure you've got something on hand for people to snack on while you get to the main event. Free-flowing alcohol and no food is a recipe for disaster.

6. NO POKING

This is a very common rookie mistake. If you poke meat on the grill, the juices will come out and your food will dry out. So using meat carvers or forks to flip your food is not recommended; go for tongs and heavy-duty spatulas.

7. DON'T SLATHER ON SAUCES UNTIL THE END

You can marinate your food before grilling to make it more flavorful. But do not coat meat with barbecue sauce during the actual cooking process. This can cause flare-ups, and the high sugar content in sauces and glazes can burn, leaving you with an inedible mess. Resist brushing until the last five minutes or so, and always feel free to re-slather once the food comes off the grill.

8. COOK EVERYTHING PROPERLY

Nothing really ruins a party like undercooked or overcooked food. When in doubt, it is always better to undercook because you can simply put the food back on the grill and continue to cook it until it is at the proper temperature. Unfortunately, once a piece of fish or a beautiful thick rib eye is overcooked, there is nothing you can do to make it moist again. See my chart (page 29) for doneness temps.

9. TAKE TIME TO REST

Not you, the food. I have said it a million times and I will say it again: Never cut into meat or fish as soon as it comes off the grill. Let the food rest and relax to allow the juices to redistribute and stay inside. I typically rest smaller cuts like fish fillets and chicken breasts for 5 minutes, thick steaks and whole chickens for 10 minutes, and large roasts for 20 minutes. Tent loosely with foil to keep warm.

10. KEEP IT CASUAL

A meal prepared outdoors on the grill invites everyone to loosen up and enjoy the party. The whole idea of grilling is to be relaxed and festive. Serve food family style on big platters, have cocktail shakers and ingredients for drinks ready to go, and lots of beer and sodas on ice so guests can help themselves. That's my kind of entertaining. Give it a try and have fun!

DURING BARBECUING OR GRILLING, real, concentrated smoky flavor comes from wood smoke, which is an integral part of cooking in a dedicated smoker. Wood chips need to be soaked for at least 30 minutes before using. Not sure what kind of wood goes with what kind of meat or fish? Here are my choices, but feel free to experiment to come up with your own personal mix.

WHERE THERE'S SMOKE, THERE'S FLAVOR

ALDER/CEDAR has a light flavor that works well with fish and poultry. Indigenous to the northwestern United States, both are the traditional wood for smoking salmon.

ALMOND gives a nutty, sweet flavor that is good with all meats. Almond is similar to pecan.

APPLE is very mild in flavor and gives food a sweetness that is especially good with poultry and pork. Note that apple will discolor chicken skin, turning it a dark brown.

CHERRY has a sweet, mild flavor that goes great with virtually everything. This is one of the most popular woods for smoking.

HICKORY adds a strong flavor to meats, so be careful not to use it to excess. It's good with beef and lamb.

MAPLE, like fruitwood, gives a sweet flavor that is excellent with poultry and ham.

MESQUITE has been very popular of late and is good for grilling, but because it burns hot and fast, it's not recommended for long barbecues. Mesquite is probably the strongest flavored wood; hence its popularity with restaurant grills that cook meat for a very short time.

OAK is strong but not overpowering and is a very good wood for beef or lamb. Oak is probably the most versatile of the hardwoods.

PECAN burns cool and provides a delicate flavor. It's a much subtler version of hickory.

WHEN IS IT DONE?

As I mentioned previously, professional chefs use the touch test to tell the doneness of meat or fish. The texture of medium-rare, for example, corresponds closely to the feel of the fleshy part of your palm below the thumb. The more the meat or fish is cooked, the less malleable it becomes. While I find that method pretty much foolproof, it does require lots of practice. So, for home cooks, I recommend using an instant-read thermometer for accuracy. It's cheap and easy to use.

Here is my chart for optimum internal doneness. The temperatures on this chart, in my opinion, keep the integrity of the meat and fish, meaning that when you cut into your meat it should be pink and juicy, not gray and dry. Fish should be moist and should flake when you break it apart with a fork. Nothing is worse than overcooked meat and fish. Why spend all that money only to be left with something resembling a piece of leather on your plate? My temperatures vary slightly from those of the USDA, so if you are serving anyone who is pregnant, old, or young or has a weakened immune system, please follow the USDA-recommended temperatures.

BEEF STEAKS & LAMB CHOPS, MEDIUM-RARE

Remove from heat	Serving temperature after resting	USDA recommends
130°F	135°F to 140°F	150°F

GROUND BEEF & LAMB, MEDIUM

Remove from heat	Serving temperature after resting	USDA recommends
135°F	140°F to 145°F	160°F

PORK TENDERLOIN & CHOPS, MEDIUM-WELL

Remove from heat	Serving temperature after resting	USDA recommends
145°F	150°F to 155°F	170°F

CHICKEN & TURKEY BREASTS, MEDIUM-WELL

Remove from heat	Serving temperature after resting	USDA recommends
150°F to 155°F	160°F	170°F

DUCK BREASTS, MEDIUM-RARE

Remove from heat	Serving temperature after resting	USDA recommends
135°F	145°F	170°F

FISH FILLETS & WHOLE FISH, MEDIUM
(red snapper, halibut, swordfish, salmon, mahimahi, and trout)

Remove from heat	Serving temperature after resting	USDA recommends
135°F	140°F to 145°F	160°F

TUNA, MEDIUM-RARE

Remove from heat	Serving temperature after resting	USDA recommends
120°F	125°F	160°F

SWEET CHERRY SLUSHY CUPS

With just a drop of alcohol, these cool cups of shaved ice and juicy cherries are as much a sweet treat to end your meal as they are a refreshing way to start it—double-duty cocktail and dessert. Cherries are one of those fantastic summer-only fruits, and when they are in season, you have to serve them as many ways as you can, whether fresh from a bowl or baked into cobbler, or muddled into a luscious, grown-ups-only slushy cup. Forget the tongue-staining slushies from your childhood; these are the real deal. **SERVES 4**

1 cup sweet cherries, pitted and halved
2 tablespoons superfine sugar
Juice of 1 fresh orange
1 teaspoon grated lemon zest
Juice of ½ lemon
2 tablespoon cherry eau-de-vie, such as kirsch
6 cups ice cubes
½ cup heavy cream, loosely whipped to very soft peaks
Fresh mint sprigs, for garnish

1 Combine the cherries, sugar, orange juice, lemon zest, lemon juice, and cherry eau-de-vie in a bowl and muddle using a muddler or a potato masher, leaving some chunks of cherry. Let sit at room temperature for at least 15 and up to 60 minutes to allow the cherries to break down and the juice to flow.
2 Put the ice cubes, in batches, in a blender or food processor and blend until crushed. Divide the ice among 4 martini glasses and top each with the cherry mixture and juices. Top each with a few tablespoons of the loosely whipped cream and a mint sprig.

BLACKBERRY MOJITOS

If you want a real taste of Cuba, you have to start with a mojito. Rum, lime juice, mint . . . you've got the drink of Hemingway in your hands. For a delicious spin on the classic, try this version. Sweet, tart, and bursting with fruity flavor, blackberries are an outstanding addition. **SERVES 2**

8 fresh mint leaves, plus more for garnish
½ cup fresh blackberries
1 tablespoon light agave syrup
Ice cubes
½ cup light rum
¼ cup fresh lime juice
Crushed ice
Lime-flavored club soda
Lime slices, for garnish

1 Add the mint leaves, blackberries, and agave syrup to a cocktail shaker. Using a muddler or the handle of a wooden spoon, muddle the ingredients until the mint is fragrant. Add the ice cubes, rum, and lime juice. Cover and shake vigorously to chill.
2 Fill 2 rocks or highball glasses with crushed ice and strain the liquid into the glasses. Top with club soda and garnish each with a slice of lime.

CALIFORNIA WHITE PEACH AND SPARKLING WINE COCKTAIL

When I see white peaches at the market, the first thing I think of is Bellinis. Forget about any version you may have had before with anything else; making this sparkling, delicate cocktail with your own puree of vanilla-scented peaches will be the only way to go from here on out. **SERVES 4 TO 6**

3 ripe white peaches
Vanilla Simple Syrup (recipe follows)
Dry California rosé sparkling wine, cold
Fresh mint sprigs, for garnish

1 Slice 1 of the peaches and set aside for garnish. Peel, pit, and chop the remaining 2 peaches, combine with the vanilla syrup in a food processor, and process until smooth.
2 Put some of the peach puree in the bottom of Champagne flutes, top with cold sparkling wine, and garnish with sliced peaches and mint sprigs.

VANILLA SIMPLE SYRUP
MAKES ½ CUP

½ cup sugar
½ vanilla bean, split and seeds scraped

Combine ½ cup water with the sugar and vanilla bean and seeds in a small saucepan, bring to a boil, and cook until the sugar is dissolved, about 2 minutes. Pour the vanilla syrup into a bowl, cover, and refrigerate until cold, at least 1 hour or overnight. Remove the vanilla bean before using.

TROPICAL SANGRIA

Citrusy lemongrass-infused simple syrup joins tart-sweet passion fruit in this deliciously refreshing white wine–based cocktail. Substituting light rum here for sangria's traditional brandy has a big tropical-flavor payoff. You can find passion fruit nectar in specialty markets and most high-end grocery stores these days. **SERVES 4 TO 6**

1 (750-ml) bottle Sauvignon Blanc, cold
1 cup passion fruit nectar
½ cup light rum
¼ to ½ cup Lemongrass Simple Syrup (recipe follows)
1 lemon, halved and thinly sliced
1 orange, halved and thinly sliced
1 bunch fresh mint, leaves only
Seeds from 1 passion fruit, optional

Combine wine, nectar, rum, simple syrup, lemon, and orange in a pitcher, cover, and refrigerate for at least 2 hours and up to 48 hours. Add mint and passion fruit seeds just before serving.

LEMONGRASS SIMPLE SYRUP
MAKES 1 CUP

1 cup sugar
1 stalk lemongrass

Combine 1 cup water and the sugar in a small saucepan. Cut the lemongrass stalk into 3 pieces and hit the stalks with the back of your knife to lightly bruise them and help release their flavor. Add the lemongrass to the pan, bring to a boil over high heat, and cook until the sugar is completely dissolved, about 2 minutes. Remove from the heat, cover, and refrigerate for at least 1 hour and up to 2 days to let the flavors develop. Strain before using.

APFELSTRUDEL COCKTAIL

As far from spiced (and spiked) apple cider as you can get, this vanilla-scented apple cocktail hits all sorts of notes, from sweet and fresh to cool and sparkling. And did I mention delicious?

SERVES 4

1 (750-ml) bottle dry sparkling wine, cold
1 cup apple juice, cold
½ cup vodka
Vanilla Simple Syrup (page 37)
1 Granny Smith apple, halved, cored, and
    thinly sliced
½ pint fresh blackberries

Pour the sparkling wine, apple juice, and vodka into a pitcher. Add the vanilla syrup, apple, and blackberries and mix to combine. Serve in champagne flutes.

VODKA GRAPE SPARKLER

Grapes, honey, and rosemary always say Greece to me. This refreshing drink is a perfect prelude to grilled meat such as lamb. Leave out the sparkling wine and vodka and you have your own homemade grape soda.

SERVES 4 TO 6

½ cup fresh lemon juice
½ cup clover honey
2 pounds seedless red grapes
¾ cup vodka, cold
1 (750-ml) bottle dry rosé sparkling
    wine, cold
Fresh rosemary sprigs

1 Combine the lemon juice and honey in a small saucepan over low heat and cook until the honey is melted. Remove from the heat and let cool.

2 Puree 1½ pounds of the grapes, in batches if needed, in a blender until smooth. Strain the mixture into a pitcher. Slice enough of the remaining grapes to make 1 cup. Add to the pitcher along with the cooled lemon juice mixture and the vodka. Refrigerate, covered, until cold, at least 1 hour.

3 Add the sparkling wine and rosemary sprigs to the pitcher just before serving. Pour into red wine goblets.

PISCO SOUR SANGRIA

Pisco is a grape brandy produced in Chile and Peru that pairs famously well with tart citrus—the frothy Pisco sour is proof positive of that. This beautiful sangria, made with a lemon-lime simple syrup and accented with thin slices of crisp green apple, sweet oranges, and tart lemons and limes, is a more food-friendly incarnation of the cocktail.

SERVES 4

1 (750-ml) bottle fruity dry white wine, such as a Sauvignon Blanc
1½ cups Pisco
1 cup fresh orange juice
½ cup Lemon-Lime Simple Syrup (recipe follows)
1 Granny Smith apple, halved, cored, and thinly sliced
1 orange, halved and thinly sliced
1 lime, thinly sliced
1 lemon, thinly sliced
1 small bunch fresh mint
Ice cubes

Mix together all the ingredients except the ice cubes in a pitcher, cover, and refrigerate for at least 4 hours or overnight. Serve in glasses over ice.

LEMON-LIME SIMPLE SYRUP
MAKES 1 CUP

1 cup sugar
2 thin lime slices
2 thin lemon slices

Combine ¾ cup water and the sugar in a small saucepan, bring to a boil over high heat, and cook until the sugar is completely dissolved, about 2 minutes. Add the lime and lemon slices, let sit at room temperature until cool, and then refrigerate for 1 hour. Remove the fruit, cover the syrup, and return to the refrigerator for up to 1 week.

LIME RICKEY FLOAT MARGARITA

Fizzy and tart, a lime rickey is the perfect refreshing treat on a summer day. This soda-shop favorite is decidedly grown up, made with deep, dark fresh cherries and of course a slug of silver tequila—this is a margarita, after all.

SERVES 4

15 fresh sour or sweet Bing cherries, pitted, plus more for garnish
¼ cup agave nectar
¼ cup maraschino liqueur
1 cup silver tequila
½ cup fresh lime juice
Lime sorbet
Lime- or cherry-flavored club soda
1 lime, cut into wedges, for garnish
Fresh mint sprigs, for garnish

1 Combine the cherries, agave nectar, and maraschino liqueur in a blender and blend a few times to coarsely chop the cherries. Transfer to a pitcher and add the tequila and lime juice. Cover and refrigerate until very cold, at least 2 hours.
2 Put a scoop of sorbet in each of 4 margarita glasses, divide the cherry mixture among the glasses, and top off with club soda. Garnish each glass with a cherry, lime wedge, and mint sprig.

WATERMELON-PLATA TEQUILA COCKTAIL

Cool and sweet watermelon always makes me feel refreshed and hydrated, and that's just from eating a juicy slice. Blend that up with tart limes and my favorite plata (silver) tequila and you've got a cocktail that can't be beat on a summer day. And what classic barbecue isn't improved by a shot of watermelon?

SERVES 8

¼ cup sugar
8 cups watermelon chunks, seeds removed
Juice of 2 limes
1½ cups fresh blueberries, plus more for garnish
½ cup lightly packed fresh mint leaves, plus more for garnish
1 cup silver tequila
Crushed ice

1 Combine ¼ cup water with the sugar in a small saucepan, bring to a boil, and cook until the sugar is dissolved, about 2 minutes. Pour the syrup into a bowl, cover, and refrigerate until cold, at least 1 hour or overnight.

2 Puree the watermelon in a food processor until smooth. Strain the juice into a bowl and discard the solids.

3 Put the syrup, lime juice, blueberries, and mint in a pitcher and muddle until the berries are slightly crushed. Add the tequila and watermelon juice and stir to combine. Refrigerate until cold, at least 1 hour.

4 Serve over crushed ice, garnished with mint leaves and blueberries.

STARTE
SALADS

RS, SIDES

DEVILED EGGS WITH *Smoked Trout* 50

GRILLED WHITE ASPARAGUS
WITH *German Green Sauce* 52

GRILLED ARTICHOKES WITH *Green Goddess Dressing* 53

GRILLED ASPARAGUS
WITH *Figs, Cabrales,* AND *Sherry Vinegar Sauce* 54

GUASACACA WITH *Tortillas Chips* 57

GRILLED BREAD SALAD
WITH *Tomatoes* AND *Green Onion Vinaigrette* 58

GRILLED WHITE ARGENTINE PIZZA 60

GRILLED SHAVED ASPARAGUS PIZZA
WITH *Robiola* AND *Parsley Oil* 63

HOMEMADE NAAN BREAD 64

FLATBREAD
WITH *Fresh Figs, Blue Cheese,* AND *Red Wine Vinaigrette* 65

GRILLED BRUSSELS SPROUTS
WITH *Hazelnut Vinaigrette* 66

GRILLED NEW CARROTS WITH *Maple* AND *Dill* 68

FIRE-ROASTED CORN
WITH *Mango-Habanero-Cilantro Butter* 69

GRILLED CORN WITH *Piquillo Pepper Butter* 71

GRILLED CORN WITH *Spicy Brown Sugar Butter* 72

EGGPLANT "CASSEROLE"
WITH *Red Pepper Pesto* AND *Cajun Bread Crumbs* 74

GRILLED MUSHROOM ESCABECHE TACOS 75

GRILLED EGGPLANT CAPONATA BRUSCHETTA
WITH *Ricotta Salata* 77

COLESLAW WITH *Creamy Cumin-Lime-Dill Vinaigrette* 78

SPANISH CAESAR SALAD
WITH *Marcona Almonds* AND *White Anchovies* 81

FIG PANZANELLA
WITH *Goat Cheese, Baby Arugula,* AND *Mint* 82

You can't go to a church social in the South without running into this classic appetizer. It's one of my favorites. The devil comes from the paprika that is always sprinkled on top. I am currently obsessed with smoked paprika, whose flavor mirrors that of the trout in this recipe. **SERVES 6 TO 8**

12 large eggs
½ cup mayonnaise
1 heaping tablespoon Dijon mustard
¼ cup finely diced Vidalia onion
4 cornichons, finely diced
3 tablespoons finely chopped fresh dill,
    plus whole sprigs for garnish
Kosher salt and freshly ground black
    pepper
1 teaspoon smoked mild paprika
½ cup shredded smoked trout, homemade
    (page 226) or store-bought
Hot sauce, optional

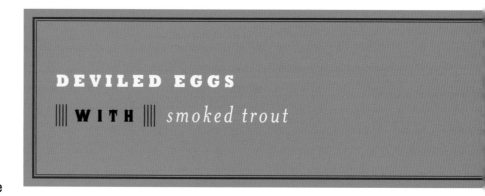

DEVILED EGGS
||| **WITH** ||| *smoked trout*

1 Put the eggs in a large saucepan, cover by 1 inch with cold water, and bring to a boil over high heat. Let boil for 1 minute, remove from the heat, cover, and let sit for 18 minutes. Drain well, put in a bowl, and cover with cold water. Let the eggs sit in the cold water for a few minutes and then drain well.

2 Once the eggs are cool, peel and slice each in half lengthwise. Put the whites on a platter and put the yolks in a medium bowl.

Add the mayonnaise, mustard, and onion to the yolks and mix until smooth. Fold in the cornichons and dill and season with salt and pepper. Divide the mixture among the whites. Cover and refrigerate for at least 30 minutes before serving.

3 Just before serving, sprinkle the tops with the smoked paprika and add a small piece of the trout to each. Drizzle with a touch of hot sauce, if desired, and garnish with dill sprigs.

Classic green sauce is normally thickened with hard-boiled eggs. This is Germany's "green sauce," or grüne sosse *(or even* salsa verde, *if you will), which is typically served with boiled root vegetables to add a touch of freshness. I like to pair it with a popular German vegetable, white asparagus, and—instead of thickening the sauce with hard-boiled eggs, as is traditional—I use the eggs as a garnish, not as part of the sauce. Use as many green herbs as you like, substituting or adding whatever is in your fridge, such as dill or tarragon.* **SERVES 4 TO 6**

½ cup crème fraîche or sour cream
¼ cup buttermilk
2 tablespoons apple cider vinegar
1 cup packed fresh flat-leaf parsley
    leaves, plus more for serving
1 cup packed watercress leaves
1 cup packed fresh spinach leaves
½ cup finely chopped fresh chives, plus
    more for serving
Kosher salt and freshly ground black
    pepper
2 pounds medium white asparagus
Canola oil
4 hard-boiled eggs, finely diced

GRILLED WHITE ASPARAGUS
||| **WITH** ||| *german green sauce*

1 Combine the crème fraîche, buttermilk, and vinegar in a food processor and process until mixed. Add the parsley, watercress, spinach, and chives and process until smooth; season with salt and pepper. Cover and refrigerate until ready to use, up to 2 hours.

2 Heat your grill to high for direct grilling (see page 23).

3 Cut off the bottom ½ inch of each asparagus spear. Using a vegetable peeler, and starting just below the tip of each spear, remove the tough peel from each spear, turning as you go. Brush the asparagus with oil and season with salt and pepper. Grill the asparagus, turning once, until lightly golden brown and just crisp-tender, about 2 minutes per side, depending on the thickness.

4 Remove to a platter, drizzle with the green sauce, and garnish with the eggs and more fresh herbs.

Talk about a dish with impact—this one is incredibly fresh and full flavored. Green goddess dressing is a California specialty that I think of as the original ranch, or at least what ranch should be. Bright lemon, a touch of garlic, and the natural salty flavor of anchovies meet parsley's baby cousin chervil, oniony chives, and the anise touch of tarragon in a creamy, altogether sensational dressing. Pour that over earthy artichokes, smoky from the grill, and you've got a seriously remarkable dish.

SERVES 4 TO 6

GRILLED ARTICHOKES
||| **WITH** ||| *green goddess dressing*

6 globe artichokes
Kosher salt
3 lemons
3 garlic cloves, minced
3 tablespoons canola oil
¼ teaspoon freshly ground black pepper
Chopped fresh herbs, such as tarragon, chives, and chervil, for garnish
Green Goddess Dressing (recipe follows)

1 Slice the tops off the artichokes, pull off the small leaves from the bottom, trim the stems, and snip off any remaining thorny tips. Bring 2 inches of water to a boil in a large pot. Add 1 tablespoon salt, the juice of 1 of the lemons, and the artichokes. Cover and steam until the artichoke bottoms pierce easily, 20 to 40 minutes, depending on their size.

2 Drain the artichokes and set aside. When cool enough to handle, cut each artichoke in half lengthwise and scrape out the fuzzy center.

3 Heat your grill to medium for direct grilling (see page 23).

4 Squeeze 2 tablespoons lemon juice from 1 of the remaining lemons into a bowl. Whisk in the garlic, oil, ½ teaspoon salt, and the pepper. Brush the artichokes with the garlic mixture and set, cut side down, on the grill. Grill, turning once, until lightly browned on both sides, 6 to 8 minutes.

5 Cut the remaining lemon into wedges. Arrange the artichokes on a platter, drizzle with some of the dressing, and garnish with the herbs and lemon wedges.

GREEN GODDESS DRESSING
MAKES ABOUT 2 CUPS

1 cup mayonnaise
½ cup crème fraîche or sour cream
1 garlic clove
Grated zest of 1 lemon
Juice of 1 lemon
2 anchovy fillets, chopped
¼ cup chopped fresh flat-leaf parsley leaves, plus more for garnish
3 fresh chives, chopped, plus more for garnish
3 tablespoons chopped fresh chervil, plus more for garnish
2 tablespoons chopped fresh tarragon, plus more for garnish
Kosher salt and freshly ground black pepper

Process the mayonnaise, crème fraîche, garlic, lemon zest, lemon juice, anchovies, and herbs in a food processor until smooth. Season with salt and pepper. Cover and refrigerate for at least 30 minutes before serving to allow the flavors to meld.

Piquant and creamy, Spanish Cabrales might be my favorite blue cheese. Sweet figs counter the savory bite of the blue-veined cheese and both find their home atop tender stalks of grilled asparagus. This is a deceptively simple dish, those three ingredients making an unexpected trinity of flavors. **SERVES 4 TO 6**

2 cups plus 1 tablespoon aged sherry
    vinegar
1 small shallot, finely diced
2 tablespoons clover honey
1 teaspoon grated orange zest
Kosher salt and freshly ground black
    pepper
2 tablespoons finely chopped fresh
    flat-leaf parsley leaves, plus more for
    garnish
24 medium asparagus spears, trimmed
3 tablespoons canola oil
12 fresh figs, quartered
8 ounces Cabrales blue cheese, crumbled
Extra-virgin olive oil

GRILLED ASPARAGUS
WITH *figs, cabrales,* AND *sherry vinegar sauce*

1 Combine 2 cups of the vinegar and the shallot in a small saucepan, bring to a boil over high heat, and cook until thickened and reduced to about ½ cup, about 30 minutes. Whisk in the honey and orange zest and season with salt and pepper. Remove from the heat and let cool to room temperature. Right before drizzling, stir in the remaining 1 tablespoon vinegar and the parsley.

2 Heat your grill to high for direct grilling (see page 23).

3 Brush the asparagus with the canola oil and season with salt and pepper. Grill until just crisp-tender, about 4 minutes. Remove to a platter. Arrange the figs around the asparagus, sprinkle the blue cheese over everything, and drizzle with the sherry vinegar sauce and a little olive oil. Garnish with chopped parsley.

Mountains of cheese and sweet onions, cooked with anchovies to add depth of flavor and enhance their savoriness, top a crisp pizza crust in this famous Argentinean dish. It has been estimated that upward of 50 percent of Argentina's population is of Italian descent, and this pizza, called fugazzeta *(a derivation of "focaccia"), is a direct reflection of that.* **SERVES 4 TO 6**

Pizza Dough (recipe follows) or 2 pounds store-bought dough
Unbleached all-purpose flour
2 tablespoons canola oil, plus more for brushing
4 brined white anchovy fillets, patted dry
¼ teaspoon red pepper flakes
3 large Vidalia or Walla Walla onions, halved and thinly sliced
1 tablespoon finely chopped fresh oregano
Kosher salt and freshly ground black pepper
2 cups grated aged fontina cheese
½ cup freshly grated Parmesan cheese

GRILLED WHITE ARGENTINE PIZZA

1 Heat your grill to high for indirect grilling (see page 23).

2 Scrape the dough onto a floured surface and cut it into 2 pieces. Shape each piece into a ball, dust with flour, and cover with plastic wrap. Let rest for 15 minutes.

3 Meanwhile, heat the oil in a large pan over medium heat. Add the anchovies and cook until melted into the oil. Add the red pepper flakes and cook for 30 seconds. Stir in the onions and cook, stirring occasionally, until they are completely soft and light blond—not caramelized. Stir in the oregano and season with salt and pepper.

4 Working with 1 ball of dough at a time, stretch or roll it out into a thin circle or rectangle. Brush with oil and season with salt and pepper. Set the dough, oiled side down, on the grill directly over the hot coals and grill until lightly golden brown, about 1 minute. Turn over and grill for 1 minute.

5 Transfer the pizza to a flat surface. Top with half of the onions and then half of the fontina. Return to the grill, this time over the cooler side (indirect heat), close the cover, and cook until the crust is golden brown and the cheese has melted, about 3 minutes.

6 Remove the pizza from the grill, sprinkle with half of the Parmesan, and cut into pieces.

7 Repeat with the remaining ball of dough. Serve hot.

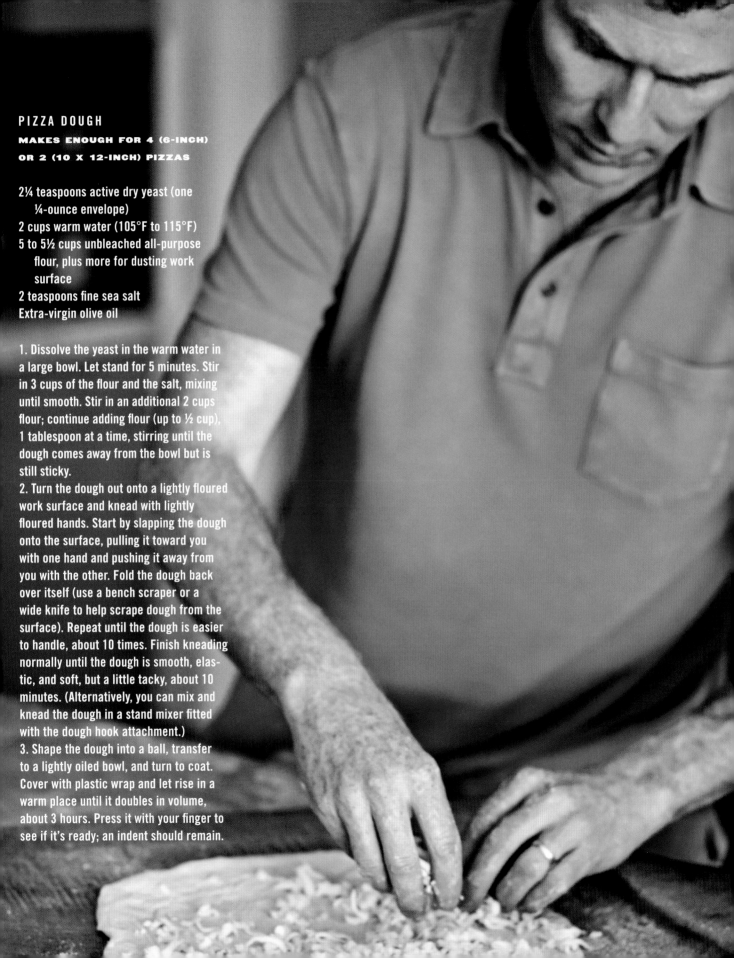

PIZZA DOUGH

MAKES ENOUGH FOR 4 (6-INCH) OR 2 (10 X 12-INCH) PIZZAS

2¼ teaspoons active dry yeast (one
    ¼-ounce envelope)
2 cups warm water (105°F to 115°F)
5 to 5½ cups unbleached all-purpose
    flour, plus more for dusting work
    surface
2 teaspoons fine sea salt
Extra-virgin olive oil

1. Dissolve the yeast in the warm water in a large bowl. Let stand for 5 minutes. Stir in 3 cups of the flour and the salt, mixing until smooth. Stir in an additional 2 cups flour; continue adding flour (up to ½ cup), 1 tablespoon at a time, stirring until the dough comes away from the bowl but is still sticky.

2. Turn the dough out onto a lightly floured work surface and knead with lightly floured hands. Start by slapping the dough onto the surface, pulling it toward you with one hand and pushing it away from you with the other. Fold the dough back over itself (use a bench scraper or a wide knife to help scrape dough from the surface). Repeat until the dough is easier to handle, about 10 times. Finish kneading normally until the dough is smooth, elastic, and soft, but a little tacky, about 10 minutes. (Alternatively, you can mix and knead the dough in a stand mixer fitted with the dough hook attachment.)

3. Shape the dough into a ball, transfer to a lightly oiled bowl, and turn to coat. Cover with plastic wrap and let rise in a warm place until it doubles in volume, about 3 hours. Press it with your finger to see if it's ready; an indent should remain.

Paper–thin asparagus ribbons (easily made with a vegetable peeler) join creamy robiola cheese on this delicate grilled pizza. This simple, delicious combination would be at home on tables across northern Italy. Verdant parsley oil, a loose mixture of olive oil, parsley, and lemon zest, adds even more bright flavor and color to this understated, elegant pizza. **SERVES 4 TO 6**

GRILLED SHAVED ASPARAGUS PIZZA ||| WITH ||| *robiola* ||| AND ||| *parsley oil*

Pizza Dough (page 61) or 2 pounds store-bought dough

Unbleached all-purpose flour

¼ cup packed fresh flat-leaf parsley leaves, finely chopped, plus more leaves for garnish

½ cup extra-virgin olive oil, plus more for drizzling

1 teaspoon grated lemon zest, plus more for garnish

Kosher salt and freshly ground black pepper

Canola oil

1 pound robiola cheese, thinly sliced

6 large asparagus spears, trimmed and thinly shaved with a vegetable peeler

½ cup freshly grated Romano cheese

1 Heat your grill to high for indirect grilling (see page 23).

2 Scrape the dough onto a floured surface and cut it into 2 pieces. Shape each piece into a ball, dust with flour, and cover with plastic wrap. Let rest for 15 minutes.

3 Meanwhile, stir together the parsley, olive oil, and lemon zest and season with salt and pepper.

4 Working with 1 ball of dough at a time, stretch or roll it out into a thin circle or rectangle. Brush with canola oil and season with salt and pepper. Set the dough, oiled side down, on the grill directly over the heat source until lightly golden brown, about 1 minute. Turn over the dough and grill for 1 minute.

5 Transfer the pizza to a flat surface. Top with half of the robiola and asparagus, drizzle with olive oil, and season with salt and pepper. Return to the grill, this time over the cooler side (indirect heat), close the cover, and cook until the crust is golden brown and the robiolo has melted, about 3 minutes.

6 Remove the pizza from the grill and drizzle with some of the parsley oil. Sprinkle with half of the Romano and some parsley leaves and lemon zest. Cut into pieces.

7 Repeat with the remaining ball of dough. Serve hot.

Forget about a knife and fork: The best utensils for eating Indian food—or other saucy, savory dishes—are your hands and a warm piece of fluffy naan. This buttery flatbread is perfect for wrapping up ingredients like an Indian taco, mopping up relishes, and taking one last swipe at your plate to clean it of delectable juices. The yogurt's role is twofold: It gives the finished bread a slight tang and tenderizes the dough for a soft final texture. **MAKES ABOUT 14 INDIVIDUAL NAANS**

2¼ teaspoons active dry yeast (one ¼-ounce envelope)
1 cup warm water (105°F to 115°F)
3 tablespoons sugar
3 tablespoons Greek yogurt
1 large egg, beaten
2 teaspoons kosher salt
4 to 4½ cups bread flour, plus more for dusting surface if kneading by hand
Canola oil
8 tablespoons (1 stick) unsalted butter, melted

HOMEMADE NAAN BREAD

1 Dissolve the yeast in the warm water in a large bowl. Let stand for about 10 minutes, until frothy. Stir in the sugar, yogurt, egg, salt, and enough of the bread flour to make a soft dough. Knead by hand for 6 to 8 minutes on a lightly floured surface, or until smooth. (Alternatively, you can mix and knead the dough in a stand mixer fitted with the dough hook attachment.) Put the dough in a well-oiled bowl, cover with a damp cloth, and set aside to rise for 1 hour, until the dough has doubled in volume.

2 Gently press down the dough and pinch off small handfuls of dough about the size of a golf ball. Roll into balls and place on a tray. Cover with a kitchen towel and allow the balls to rise until doubled in size, about 30 minutes.

3 Meanwhile, heat your grill to high for direct grilling (see page 23).

4 Roll out 1 ball of dough into a thin circle. Lightly oil the grill and brush the dough on one side with butter. Put the dough on the grill, butter side down, and cook for 2 to 3 minutes, or until puffy and lightly browned. Brush the uncooked side with butter, turn over the bread, and cook until browned, 2 to 4 minutes. Remove the bread from the grill and continue the process until all the naans have been prepared.

With their delicate, honeyed taste and lush texture, fresh California figs are shown off in all their glory atop this delicate flatbread. Smooth Monterey Jack cheese anchors the figs, and pungent blue cheese highlights the fruit's sweet nature with its salty tang. Fruity California red wine, reduced with lemony thyme and anisette-flavored fennel seeds, transforms into a glossy vinaigrette to finish it all off.

SERVES 4

FLATBREAD ||| WITH ||| *fresh figs,* *blue cheese,* ||| AND ||| *red wine vinaigrette*

Pizza Dough (page 61) or 2 pounds
   store-bought dough
Unbleached all-purpose flour
Canola oil
**Kosher salt and freshly ground black
   pepper**
1¼ cups grated Monterey Jack cheese
**1 pint fresh ripe figs, stemmed and
   halved**
4 ounces blue cheese, crumbled
**Reduced Red Wine Vinaigrette (recipe
   follows)**
Fresh flat-leaf parsley leaves

REDUCED RED WINE VINAIGRETTE
MAKES ABOUT ¾ CUP

2 cups fruity dry red wine
4 fresh thyme sprigs
¼ teaspoon black peppercorns
¼ teaspoon fennel seeds
1 tablespoon rice vinegar
Kosher salt
½ cup extra-virgin olive oil
Clover honey

1 Heat your grill to high for indirect grilling (see page 23).

2 Scrape the dough onto a floured surface and cut it into 2 pieces. Shape each piece into a ball, dust with flour, and cover with plastic wrap. Let rest for 15 minutes.

3 Working with 1 ball of dough at a time, stretch or roll it out into a thin circle or rectangle. Brush with canola oil and season with salt and pepper. Set the dough, oiled side down, on the grill directly over the heat source and grill until lightly golden brown, about 1 minute. Turn over the dough and grill for 1 minute.

4 Transfer the flatbread to a flat surface. Top with half of the Monterey Jack. Arrange half of the cut figs on top and half of the blue cheese around the figs. Return to the grill, this time over the cooler side (indirect heat), close the cover, and cook until the crust is golden brown, the cheeses have melted, and the figs are heated through, 3 minutes.

5 Remove the flatbread from the grill, drizzle with some of the red wine vinaigrette, and garnish with parsley leaves. Cut into pieces.

6 Repeat with the remaining ball of dough. Serve hot.

1. Boil the wine, thyme, peppercorns, and fennel seeds in a small saucepan over high heat until reduced to ¼ cup. Strain into a blender; discard the solids.

2. Add the vinegar, season with salt, and blend to combine. With the motor running, slowly add the oil and blend until emulsified. Season with honey to taste.

Tender on the inside and slightly charred and crisp leaved on the outside, these little cabbages are transformed by just a few minutes on the grill into a surprisingly dynamic dish. The grill's high heat does more than blister the sprouts' outer leaves for a great bit of texture; it also lends a somewhat nutty taste that's echoed in the rich hazelnut–studded vinaigrette. **SERVES 4 TO 6**

1 pound medium Brussels sprouts, stems trimmed and outer leaves removed
Kosher salt and freshly ground black pepper
¼ cup white wine vinegar
1 tablespoon finely diced shallot
1 tablespoon clover honey
2 teaspoons Dijon mustard
½ cup extra-virgin olive oil
Canola oil
3 tablespoons finely chopped toasted hazelnuts
1 teaspoon grated orange zest

GRILLED BRUSSELS SPROUTS
||| **WITH** ||| *hazelnut vinaigrette*

1 Heat your grill to high for direct grilling (see page 23). If using wooden skewers, soak them in cold water for at least 15 minutes.

2 Bring a large pot of salted water to a boil over high heat. Add the Brussels sprouts and cook until crisp-tender (a skewer inserted into the center of a sprout meets a little resistance), about 5 minutes. Drain, rinse under cold water, and drain well again. Pat dry with paper towels.

3 Whisk together the vinegar, shallot, honey, mustard, and salt and pepper to taste in a medium bowl. Slowly whisk in the olive oil until the vinaigrette is emulsified.

4 Toss the Brussels sprouts with a few tablespoons of canola oil and season with salt and pepper. Thread the sprouts onto the skewers and grill on both sides until golden brown and slightly charred and just tender, about 2 minutes per side. Remove the Brussels sprouts to a cutting board and cut them in half. Transfer to a platter.

5 Drizzle the vinaigrette over the warm Brussels sprouts and top with the hazelnuts and orange zest.

Carrots might not be the first vegetable that comes to mind as a good fit for the grill, but trust me on this one. The pairing of smoke with the root vegetable's natural sweetness and the addition of maple syrup and dill may just become a new classic American side dish—at least it will at my barbecues.

SERVES 4 TO 6

Kosher salt and freshly ground black
    pepper
1 bunch farm-stand carrots, green tops
    trimmed to about ½ inch
2 tablespoons unsalted butter
½ cup pure grade B maple syrup
3 tablespoons chopped fresh dill

GRILLED NEW CARROTS
||| WITH |||
maple ||| **AND** ||| *dill*

1 Heat your grill to high for direct grilling (see page 23).

2 Bring a large pot of salted water to a boil, add the carrots, and cook until a paring knife inserted into the center of a carrot meets with slight resistance, about 3 minutes. Drain and immediately rinse with cold water to stop the cooking. Drain well again and pat dry with paper towels.

3 Melt the butter in a small saucepan, add the maple syrup, and stir until combined. Brush the carrots with some of the glaze and season with salt and pepper. Grill until golden brown on all sides and just cooked through, about 2 minutes. Remove the carrots to a platter, brush the tops with more of the glaze, and sprinkle with the chopped fresh dill.

Removing the corn silks before soaking the corn and then cooking the corn over a medium flame allows it to grill and steam at once. The husks won't burn due to the soaking, but they do allow the heat to come through and slightly caramelize the sweet kernels. Mango and honey bring out that sweetness and temper the hit of heat that a fiery habanero brings to the mix.

SERVES 6

FIRE-ROASTED CORN
||| WITH |||
mango-habanero-cilantro butter

¼ cup mango nectar or orange juice
2 tablespoons clover honey
1 habanero chile, halved
2 ripe mangoes, peeled, pitted, and coarsely chopped
¾ pound (3 sticks) unsalted butter, slightly softened
¼ cup tightly packed fresh cilantro leaves
Kosher salt
12 ears of corn

1 Combine the mango nectar, honey, and habanero in a medium saucepan over high heat and bring to a boil. Add the mangoes and cook, stirring occasionally, until very soft and the liquid is absorbed, about 15 minutes. Transfer the mixture to a food processor and process until smooth. Strain into a bowl and let cool to room temperature. Discard the liquid.

2 Return the mango puree to the food processor with the butter, cilantro, and 1 teaspoon salt and process until smooth. Scrape the butter into a bowl, cover, and refrigerate until chilled.

3 Heat your grill to medium for direct grilling (see page 23).

4 Pull the outer husks down each ear of corn to the base. Strip away the silk from each ear of corn. Fold the husks back into place and tie the ends together with kitchen string. Place the ears of corn in a large bowl of cold water with 1 tablespoon salt for 10 minutes.

5 Remove the corn from the water and shake off the excess. Put the corn on the grill, close the cover, and grill, turning every 5 minutes, for 15 to 20 minutes, or until the kernels are tender when pierced with a paring knife.

6 Peel back the husks and serve the corn hot, slathered with the mango butter.

The sweet, slightly piquant piquillo pepper, sold roasted and jarred, tastes much like a roasted red pepper but more intensely so, as well as having a slight smoky edge. Its flavor is a great match for simply grilled corn, sweet enhancing sweet and yet not so much so that the tang is lost. This garlicky butter will have you licking your fingertips; it's addictively good. **SERVES 4 TO 6**

GRILLED CORN
⦀ WITH ⦀ *piquillo pepper butter*

½ pound (2 sticks) unsalted butter, slightly softened
4 jarred piquillo peppers, patted dry and chopped
4 garlic cloves, chopped
2 teaspoons chopped fresh thyme
1 teaspoon mild Spanish paprika
Kosher salt
¼ teaspoon freshly ground black pepper
12 ears of corn

1 Combine the butter, piquillo peppers, garlic, thyme, paprika, 1 teaspoon salt, and the pepper in a food processor and process until smooth. Scrape the butter into a bowl, cover, and refrigerate for at least 1 hour and up to 24 hours. Let soften slightly before using.

2 Heat your grill to high for direct grilling (see page 23).

3 Pull the outer husks down each ear of corn to the base. Strip away the silk from each ear of corn. Fold the husks back into place and tie the ends together with kitchen string. Place the ears of corn in a large bowl of cold water with 1 tablespoon salt for 10 minutes.

4 Remove the corn from the water and shake off the excess. Put the corn on the grill, close the cover, and grill, turning every 5 minutes, for 15 to 20 minutes, or until the kernels are tender when pierced with a paring knife.

5 Peel back the husks and serve the corn hot, slathered with the piquillo butter.

Just the right touch of brown sugar emphasizes and enhances the already sweet nature of golden corn on the cob and makes for a gorgeous final dish as it caramelizes on the grill. Spicy cayenne and complex allspice drive home the Caribbean flavors in this savory recipe; tart lime juice and an extra sprinkling of crunchy kosher salt make this corn really pop. **SERVES 4 TO 6**

½ pound (2 sticks) unsalted butter,
    slightly softened
3 tablespoons packed light brown sugar
1 teaspoon ground allspice
⅛ teaspoon cayenne
Kosher salt, plus more for serving
12 ears of corn
Lime wedges
Finely chopped fresh cilantro leaves,
    optional

GRILLED CORN
||| **WITH** ||| *spicy brown sugar butter*

1 Combine the butter, brown sugar, allspice, cayenne, and ½ teaspoon salt in a bowl and mix until combined. Cover and refrigerate for at least 1 hour and up to 2 days to allow the flavors to meld. Let soften slightly before using.

2 Heat your grill to high for direct grilling (see page 23).

3 Pull the outer husks down each ear of corn to the base. Strip away the silk from each ear of corn. Fold the husks back into place and tie the ends together with kitchen string. Place the ears of corn in a large bowl of cold water with 1 tablespoon salt for 10 minutes.

4 Remove the corn from the water and shake off the excess. Put the corn on the grill, close the cover, and grill, turning every 5 minutes, for 10 to 15 minutes, or until the kernels are almost tender when pierced with a paring knife.

5 Peel back the husks. Brush the corn with some of the spicy butter and return to the grill. Grill on all sides until lightly caramelized, 1 to 2 minutes.

6 Remove the corn from the grill and brush with more of the butter and sprinkle with salt. Serve with lime wedges for squeezing on top and garnish with cilantro, if desired.

A Louisiana take on eggplant Parmesan, this dish is a lighter remake with grilled as opposed to fried eggplant. Red pepper pesto—rich with fire-roasted flavor from the bell peppers, a natural saltiness from Romano cheese, and nutty, buttery pine nuts—makes a delectable layer of flavor between meaty eggplant slices and creamy mozzarella. A sprinkling of toasted bread crumbs adds crunch without frying and the Cajun seasonings (you can use some reserved from the Cajun Brined Turkey, Two Ways, page 136) create a continuity of flavor across the board of any Louisiana meal. **SERVES 6**

EGGPLANT "CASSEROLE"
WITH *red pepper pesto* AND *cajun bread crumbs*

TOPPING

¼ cup canola oil

2 garlic cloves, smashed to a paste

1 teaspoon mild Spanish paprika

Pinch of cayenne

6 slices day-old Italian bread, crusts removed, coarsely ground in food processor (about 1¼ cups)

3 tablespoons finely chopped fresh flat-leaf parsley leaves

2 teaspoons chopped fresh thyme

Kosher salt and freshly ground black pepper

EGGPLANT

8 baby Italian eggplants, sliced lengthwise

Canola oil

Kosher salt and freshly ground black pepper

4 grilled or jarred roasted red bell peppers, peeled, seeded, and chopped

2 garlic cloves, finely chopped

3 tablespoons pine nuts

1 tablespoon fresh oregano leaves

½ cup extra-virgin olive oil

¼ cup freshly grated Romano cheese

1 pound fresh mozzarella, thinly sliced

1 Make the topping: Heat the canola oil in a medium sauté pan over medium heat. Add the garlic and cook for 30 seconds. Add the paprika and cayenne and cook for 30 seconds. Add the bread crumbs and cook, stirring occasionally, until lightly golden brown, about 5 minutes. Remove the bread crumbs from the heat, add the parsley and thyme, and season with salt and pepper.

2 Grill the eggplant: Heat your grill to high for direct grilling (see page 23).

3 Brush the eggplant with canola oil on both sides and season with salt and pepper. Grill until lightly golden brown and just cooked through, about 3 minutes per side. Remove to a plate.

4 Combine the roasted peppers, garlic, pine nuts, and oregano in a food processor and process until coarsely chopped. With the motor running, slowly add the olive oil and process until emulsified. Add the Romano, season with salt and pepper, and pulse a few times to incorporate.

5 In a 9 x 11-inch ceramic baking dish (not glass), layer the eggplant slices with the red pepper pesto and mozzarella, ending with a layer of the cheese. Top with some of the bread crumbs. Put the dish on a baking sheet and place on the grates of the grill. Close the cover and bake until the cheese has melted, about 15 minutes.

"Escabeche" originally referred to a Spanish dish of fish or meat cooked and pickled in a hot acidic bath. Its New World translation is more liberal and encompasses all sorts of ingredients, like these meaty portobello mushrooms. Excellent in tacos as a vegetarian option, these versatile mushrooms would also be good paired with steak and chicken. Earthy and flavorful, they are delicious as is and a great addition to a relish tray. **SERVES 4**

GRILLED MUSHROOM ESCABECHE TACOS

1 Prepare the mushrooms: Combine the vinegar, sugar, garlic, serrano, onion, allspice, cloves, cinnamon, thyme, and 1 tablespoon salt in a medium saucepan. Bring to a boil and cook until the sugar and salt have dissolved, about 1 minute. Remove this pickling liquid from the heat and let cool to room temperature. Whisk in the olive oil.

2 Heat your grill to high for direct grilling (see page 23).

3 Brush the mushroom caps on both sides with canola oil and season with salt and pepper. Grill the caps until golden brown, slightly charred, and just cooked through, about 4 minutes per side. Remove the mushrooms, cut each cap into ¼-inch-thick slices, and add to the pickling liquid. Stir in the cilantro and oregano. Let sit at room temperature for 30 minutes and up to 4 hours.

4 Make the tacos: Wrap the tortillas in a damp cloth, wrap the cloth in foil, and heat on the grill with the cover closed for 5 minutes. Remove and grill each tortilla for 10 seconds on each side.

5 Lay the tortillas flat, top with a few slices of mushroom, some of the red onion from the pickled mixture, some tomato, radish, watercress, and goat cheese. Fold over each tortilla and eat.

MUSHROOMS

2 cups aged sherry vinegar
2 tablespoons sugar
2 garlic cloves, thinly sliced
1 serrano chile, thinly sliced
1 small red onion, thinly sliced
6 allspice berries
3 whole cloves
1 cinnamon stick
4 fresh thyme sprigs
Kosher salt and freshly ground black pepper
¼ cup extra-virgin olive oil
6 portobello mushrooms, stems and gills removed
½ cup canola oil
2 tablespoons finely chopped fresh cilantro leaves
1 tablespoon finely chopped fresh oregano

TACOS

12 (6-inch) corn tortillas
1 ripe beefsteak tomato, seeded and finely diced
4 radishes, thinly sliced
1 small bunch watercress
8 ounces soft fresh goat cheese, crumbled

Sicilians love a savory dish that hits both sweet and sour notes. Eggplant is especially good at picking up the flavors of whatever it is paired with, and in this case it absorbs the dynamic mix of ingredients from sweet golden raisins to briny green olives. This is a great make-ahead dish because it tastes best after sitting for at least an hour so that all those pungent flavors can marry. **SERVES 4 TO 6**

GRILLED EGGPLANT CAPONATA BRUSCHETTA
||| **WITH** ||| *ricotta salata*

1 large eggplant, cut into ¾-inch-thick slices
4 plum tomatoes
¼ cup plus 2 tablespoons canola oil
Kosher salt and freshly ground black pepper
1 large celery stalk, finely diced
1 small red onion, halved and thinly sliced
Pinch of red pepper flakes
1 cup white wine vinegar
¼ cup sugar
1 cup Sicilian green olives, pitted and chopped
¼ cup golden raisins
2 tablespoons brined capers, drained
¼ cup chopped fresh flat-leaf parsley leaves
¼ cup chopped fresh basil leaves
1 loaf ciabatta, halved lengthwise
Extra-virgin olive oil
4 ounces ricotta salata cheese, grated

1 Heat your grill to high for direct grilling (see page 23).

2 Brush the eggplant and tomatoes with ¼ cup of the canola oil and season with salt and pepper. Grill the eggplant until golden brown and cooked through, about 4 minutes per side. Grill the tomatoes until charred all over, about 8 minutes. Remove both to a cutting board and cut into dice.

3 Heat the remaining 2 tablespoons canola oil in a large sauté pan over medium-high heat. Add the celery, red onion, and red pepper flakes and cook until soft, about 5 minutes. Add the vinegar and sugar and boil until slightly reduced, about 5 minutes. Add the eggplant, tomato, olives, and raisins and simmer for 5 minutes. Remove from the heat and stir in the capers, parsley, and basil and season with salt and pepper. Transfer to a bowl and let sit at room temperature for at least 1 hour before serving. (The caponata can be made 1 day in advance and stored, covered, in the refrigerator. Bring to room temperature before serving.)

4 Grill the bread on both sides until slightly charred, about 30 seconds per side. Remove from the grill, drizzle with olive oil, and season with salt and pepper. Top each half with some of the eggplant caponata and sprinkle with ricotta salata. Slice crosswise into 1-inch-thick slices to serve.

Crunchy coleslaw is a great accompaniment that brings some levity and a change of texture to barbecued meats. Herbaceous dill and tangy lime juice balance the warm, earthy notes of toasted cumin in a creamy vinaigrette for shreds of sweet carrots, delicate Napa cabbage, and vibrant red and yellow bell peppers. This is a surprisingly versatile coleslaw recipe; it works just as well with Mexican and Southwestern cuisines as it does with Southeast Asian.

SERVES 4 TO 6

½ cup mayonnaise
Grated zest of 1 lime
¼ cup fresh lime juice
1 teaspoon celery salt
½ teaspoon cumin seeds, toasted
1 tablespoon sugar
¼ cup chopped fresh dill
Kosher salt and freshly ground
    black pepper
1 head Napa cabbage, finely
    shredded
1 large carrot, julienned
1 red bell pepper, julienned
1 yellow bell pepper, julienned
1 small red onion, halved and
    thinly sliced

COLESLAW ||| WITH |||
creamy cumin–lime–dill vinaigrette

1 Whisk together the mayonnaise, lime zest, lime juice, celery salt, cumin seeds, sugar, and dill in a large bowl and season with kosher salt and pepper.

2 Add the cabbage, carrot, bell peppers, and onion and toss to coat in the dressing; season with kosher salt and pepper. Cover and refrigerate for at least 1 hour and up to 4 hours before serving.

A ubiquitous dish that's fun to riff on, the Caesar salad is always a crowd-pleaser. This version features some fantastic Spanish ingredients, including sweet and delicate Marcona almonds, nutty Manchego cheese, and, my favorite, white anchovies. The brined meaty anchovies, or **boquerones,** *are milder and fresher than any salt-packed variety. If you think you don't like anchovies, give these sweet fillets a try.*

SERVES 4

SPANISH CAESAR SALAD

WITH *marcona almonds* AND *white anchovies*

1 teaspoon grated orange zest
2 tablespoons fresh orange juice
2 tablespoons red wine or sherry vinegar
2 tablespoons mayonnaise
2 teaspoons Dijon mustard
1 teaspoon smoked mild paprika, plus more for garnish
½ teaspoon hot sauce
2 garlic cloves, chopped
Kosher salt and freshly ground black pepper
½ cup canola oil
1 large head romaine lettuce leaves
1 (15.5-ounce) can chickpeas, drained, rinsed well, and drained again
½ cup Marcona almonds
10 brined white anchovy fillets, patted dry
¼ cup fresh flat-leaf parsley leaves
2 ounces Manchego cheese, shaved

1 Combine the orange zest, orange juice, vinegar, mayonnaise, mustard, paprika, hot sauce, and garlic in a blender and blend until smooth. Season with salt and pepper. With the motor running, slowly add the oil and blend until the dressing is smooth.

2 Remove 6 of the romaine leaves and arrange on a platter. Chop the remaining leaves into bite-sized pieces and put in a bowl with the chickpeas. Add half of the dressing and toss to coat; season with salt and pepper.

3 Arrange the dressed salad over the whole leaves and scatter the almonds, anchovies, and parsley over the top. Drizzle with more of the dressing before topping with the Manchego and a sprinkling of paprika.

This sweet–and–savory bread salad is bursting with summery flavor. A blend of peppery arugula, fragrant basil, and refreshing mint laces the salad with green, fresh flavor while sweet balsamic echoes the honeyed taste of delicate fresh figs. Tangy goat cheese highlights the flavors already in play and finishes the dish with a rich touch.

SERVES 4 TO 6

8 fresh figs, quartered
½ cup balsamic vinegar
6 (½-inch-thick) slices day-old Tuscan bread
¼ cup canola oil
Kosher salt and freshly ground black pepper
1 small shallot, finely diced
½ cup extra-virgin olive oil
4 ounces baby arugula
¼ cup fresh mint leaves, torn
¼ cup fresh basil leaves, torn
4 ounces fresh goat cheese, crumbled

FIG PANZANELLA ||| WITH |||
goat cheese, baby arugula, ||| AND ||| mint

1 Combine the figs and vinegar in a bowl and let sit at room temperature for 30 minutes. Remove the figs and reserve the vinegar.

2 Heat your grill to high for direct grilling (see page 23).

3 Brush both sides of the bread with the canola oil and season with salt and pepper. Grill until golden brown and slightly charred on both sides, about 40 seconds per side. Remove the bread, let cool slightly, and cut into 1-inch pieces.

4 Add the shallot to the reserved vinegar, season with salt and pepper, and whisk in the olive oil.

5 Combine the bread, arugula, mint, and, basil in a large bowl. Add half of the dressing and toss to combine. Transfer to a large platter, top with the figs and goat cheese, and drizzle with the remaining dressing; season with salt and pepper. Let the salad sit at room temperature for at least 20 minutes before serving.

Go to Mexico and you will find vendors, either with carts in the city or baskets on the beaches, selling cups of fresh fruits and vegetables served up with a squeeze of lime, a sprinkling of salt, and a dash of chile powder. The combination may seem odd at first to the American palate, but the combination of sweet, sour, salty, and spicy is addictive. Grilling mango intensifies its natural honeyed sweetness, adding another dimension to a simple but powerful play of flavors. **SERVES 4**

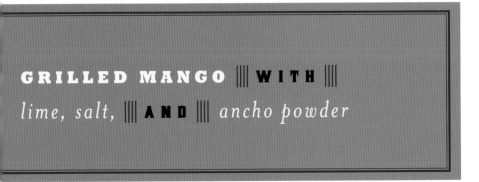

GRILLED MANGO ||| WITH |||
lime, salt, ||| **AND** ||| *ancho powder*

Grated zest of 1 lime
1 teaspoon fine sea salt
¼ teaspoon ancho chile powder
4 ripe mangoes, halved and pitted
2 tablespoons canola oil
Juice of 1 lime

1 Heat your grill to medium for direct grilling (see page 23).
2 Combine the lime zest, salt, and ancho powder in a small bowl.
3 Brush the mangoes on both sides with the oil and grill, cut side down, until slightly charred, about 1 minute. Flip over the mangoes and continue grilling until slightly charred, about 1 minute longer.

4 Remove the mangoes from the grill. Using a sharp paring knife, evenly score the flesh of each half lengthwise 3 times and then crosswise 3 or 4 times; do not cut all the way through the peel. Turn the flesh inside out so that the mango cubes stick out. Transfer to a platter and drizzle with the lime juice and sprinkle with the ancho mixture.

I start so many dishes with savory, pungent onions to create a depth of flavor that can't be beat. But onions do not need to be simply an ingredient in a dish—in this case, they are the dish. Sweet Vidalias, mild to begin with, become even more mellow as they roast on the grill. A hearty relish full of smoky, salty bacon and fresh, assertive green onions pulls everything into focus. **SERVES 6**

6 Vidalia onions, peeled
2 tablespoons plus 1 teaspoon canola oil
2 garlic cloves, chopped
2 tablespoons ancho chile powder
1 tablespoon sweet paprika
½ teaspoon chile de árbol powder or
  cayenne
1½ cups ketchup
1 heaping tablespoon Dijon mustard
1 tablespoon red wine vinegar
1 tablespoon Worcestershire sauce
1 canned chipotle in adobo, chopped
2 tablespoons packed dark brown sugar
1 tablespoon clover honey
1 tablespoon molasses
Kosher salt and freshly ground pepper
1½ cups vegetable stock
½ pound thick-cut bacon, finely diced
2 tablespoons finely chopped fresh
  flat-leaf parsley leaves
3 green onions, white and green parts,
  finely chopped

WHOLE "ROASTED" VIDALIA ONIONS ‖ WITH ‖ *bacon* **‖ AND ‖** *green onion relish*

1 Slice the tops off each onion and hollow out the onions, leaving about a ½-inch shell. Slice a little off the bottom of each onion so that the onions sit flat. Chop the onion centers and reserve ½ cup for the barbecue sauce.

2 Heat 2 tablespoons of the oil over medium-high heat in a heavy-bottomed medium saucepan. Add the ½ cup chopped onions and cook until soft, 3 to 4 minutes. Add the garlic and cook for 1 minute. Add the ancho, paprika, and chile de árbol and cook for 1 minute. Add the ketchup and ½ cup water, bring to a boil, and simmer for 5 minutes. Add the mustard, vinegar, Worcestershire, chipotle, brown sugar, honey, and molasses and simmer, stirring occasionally, for 10 minutes until thickened.

3 Transfer the mixture to a food processor and puree until smooth; season with salt and pepper to taste. Pour into a bowl and allow to cool to room temperature. The barbecue sauce will keep for 1 week in the refrigerator stored in a tightly sealed container.

4 Heat your grill to high for indirect grilling (see page 23).

5 Put the onion shells in a disposable aluminum pan and add the vegetable stock to the bottom. Fill the cavities with the barbecue sauce and put the pan on the cooler side of the grill (indirect heat). Cover the grill and cook until the onions are soft but still hold their shape, about 30 minutes.

6 While the onions are cooking, heat the remaining 1 teaspoon canola oil in a medium sauté pan over medium heat. Add the bacon and cook, stirring occasionally, until the fat is rendered and the bacon is crisp, about 10 minutes. Stir in the parsley and green onions and season with pepper.

7 Transfer the onions to a platter and sprinkle the tops with the bacon and green onion relish.

Jicama and radish have similar textures, crisp and refreshing, two words that are in turn a perfect way to sum up this light salad. Whereas jicama has a mild sweetness, radish is sharp and peppery, and the two play beautifully off each other. Spicy, fruity fresh ginger adds warmth to the sweet-sour-bitter grapefruit and, of course, honey mellows both in this bright vinaigrette, which coats the crunch in flavor.

SERVES 4

JICAMA-RADISH SALAD
||| WITH |||
grapefruit-ginger vinaigrette

1½ cups pink grapefruit juice
1 tablespoon clover honey, or more if
    needed
2 tablespoons rice vinegar
2 teaspoons finely grated fresh ginger
1 teaspoon finely chopped fresh thyme
Kosher salt and freshly ground black
    pepper
½ cup canola oil
1 ripe Hass avocado, peeled, pitted, and
    diced
½ small jicama, peeled and cut into
    julienne
1 carrot, cut into julienne
4 large radishes, cut into julienne
¼ cup fresh flat-leaf parsley leaves

1 Put the grapefruit juice in a small nonreactive saucepan and boil over high heat until reduced to about ¼ cup. Transfer to a bowl, add the honey, and let cool slightly. Whisk in the rice vinegar, ginger, and thyme and season with salt and pepper. Slowly whisk in the oil until emulsified.

2 Combine the avocado, jicama, carrot, and radishes in a large bowl. Add the grapefruit vinaigrette and toss to coat; season with salt and pepper. Cover and refrigerate for at least 1 hour and up to 8 hours. Add the parsley just before serving.

I love to put stone fruit on the grill; the heat turns any piece of less-than-ripe fruit (which is what you should start with here, actually) into the best version of itself. Perfect white peaches are full of aromatic sweetness, untouched by acidity; grilling brings out these qualities even more. A spoonful of fresh and nutty pesto with a touch of heat makes these seasonal beauties into a fantastic side dish.

SERVES 4 TO 6

1½ cups packed fresh flat-leaf parsley
    leaves
½ cup packed fresh mint leaves
½ cup sliced almonds, lightly toasted
    (see page 202), plus more for garnish
1 garlic clove, chopped
1 serrano chile, chopped
Grated zest of 1 lime
½ cup extra-virgin olive oil
Kosher salt and freshly ground black
    pepper
5 just-underripe white peaches, halved
    and pitted
2 tablespoons canola oil

GRILLED CALIFORNIA WHITE PEACHES
||| WITH ||| *almond-mint pesto*

1 Combine parsley, mint, almonds, garlic, serrano, and lime zest in a food processor and process until coarsely chopped. With the motor running, slowly add the olive oil and season with salt and pepper. If the pesto is too thick to pour, add a little water.

2 Heat your grill to high for direct grilling (see page 23).

3 Brush the cut side of the peaches with canola oil and grill until golden brown and caramelized, about 1½ minutes. Flip over the peaches and continue grilling until just heated through, about 1 minute.

4 Arrange the peach halves on a platter and drizzle with the pesto. Garnish with sliced almonds.

Cubanelle and Anaheim chiles are both thin-walled peppers that are just made for stuffing. Filled with a salty, herb-flecked cheese filling and grilled, they are a perfect side dish for grilled lamb or beef main courses. To keep the flavors authentic with Greek recipes, use your charcoal grill, if you have one. **SERVES 4 TO 6**

8 ounces Greek feta cheese, patted dry
    and crumbled
8 ounces ricotta cheese
2 garlic cloves, finely chopped
¼ cup plus 2 tablespoons freshly grated
    Romano cheese
1 large egg
1 teaspoon grated lemon zest
1 teaspoon dried oregano
¼ cup finely chopped fresh dill
Pinch of red pepper flakes
Kosher salt and freshly ground black
    pepper
6 Anaheim or cubanelle chiles, halved
    lengthwise, seeded, and stemmed
¼ cup canola oil

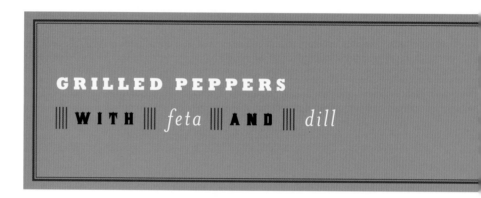

GRILLED PEPPERS
WITH *feta* AND *dill*

1 Stir together the feta, ricotta, garlic, ¼ cup of the Romano, the egg, lemon zest, oregano, dill, and red pepper flakes; season with salt and pepper. Cover and refrigerate for at least 1 hour and up to 24 hours to allow the flavors to meld. Remove the mixture from the refrigerator 30 minutes before using. Transfer the mixture to a pastry bag.

2 Heat your grill to high for direct grilling (see page 23). If you have a vegetable basket or grill topper (see Sources), place it on the grill.

3 Brush the chiles inside and outside with canola oil and season with salt and pepper. Fill the chiles with the feta mixture and sprinkle the tops with the remaining 2 tablespoons Romano. Arrange the chiles on the basket or topper, if using; close the cover and grill until the chiles are soft and the filling is lightly golden brown, about 15 minutes. Serve hot or at room temperature.

This is not a chowder at all, but rather a salad composed of the soup's star ingredients—a fantastic way to shine the spotlight on sweet summer corn and thin-skinned, tender new potatoes. Forget just a base note; salty, smoky bacon moves into a starring role. The vinaigrette is made with the bacon's fat, scenting the whole dish with its delectable flavor, while the crisp-cooked bacon is scattered atop the dish with a green hit of chives. **SERVES 4 TO 6**

NEW POTATO-CORN CHOWDER SALAD

3 pounds red new potatoes
Kosher salt and freshly ground black pepper
4 tablespoons canola oil
12 ounces slab bacon, diced
1 small red onion, halved and thinly sliced
8 ears of corn, kernels cut from the cobs
½ cup apple cider vinegar
2 teaspoons clover honey
Few dashes of hot sauce
2 tablespoons finely chopped fresh chives

1 Put the potatoes in a large pot, cover with cold water by 2 inches, and add 2 tablespoons salt. Bring to a boil and cook until the potatoes are fork-tender, 15 to 25 minutes, depending on their size. Drain well and let cool for 5 minutes. Cut into a medium dice and put in a large bowl.

2 While the potatoes are cooking, heat 2 tablespoons of the oil in a large sauté pan over medium heat. Add the bacon and cook until crispy and the fat has rendered, about 10 minutes. Remove the bacon with a slotted spoon to a plate lined with paper towels.

3 Add the remaining 2 tablespoons oil to the rendered bacon fat and heat until the mixture begins to shimmer. Add the onion to the pan and cook over medium heat until soft, about 5 minutes. Add the corn and cook for 2 minutes.

4 Add ¼ cup water, the vinegar, honey, and hot sauce and bring to a boil. Season with salt and pepper and immediately pour over the warm potatoes. Gently toss to combine. Top with the crispy bacon and the chives. Serve warm or at room temperature.

Crabmeat-stuffed or twice-baked potatoes are a favorite in the Deep South, and while I love the concept—I just adore shellfish in any preparation—I do find them to be a bit heavy for every occasion. This grilled version is mouthwateringly delicious and—lacking the sour cream, cream cheese, or heavy cream and cheese the traditional recipe calls for—quite a bit lighter. A couple of tablespoons of mayonnaise make the dressing just a tiny bit creamy and pungent green onions add tons of flavor and a shot of color to the sweet crab mixture. **SERVES 6**

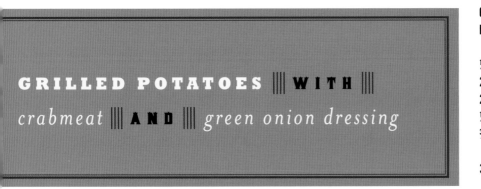

GRILLED POTATOES ||| WITH |||
crabmeat ||| **AND** ||| *green onion dressing*

6 russet potatoes, scrubbed
Kosher salt and freshly ground black
   pepper
¼ cup white wine vinegar
2 tablespoons mayonnaise
2 tablespoons Dijon mustard
½ cup canola oil, plus more for brushing
¾ pound jumbo lump crabmeat,
   picked over
3 green onions, green and pale green
   parts, thinly sliced
¼ cup chopped fresh flat-leaf parsley
   leaves
Cayenne

1 Put the potatoes in a large pot, cover with cold water by 2 inches, and add 2 tablespoons salt. Bring to a boil and cook until a knife inserted into the center of a potato meets with some resistance, 25 to 35 minutes, depending on the size. Drain and let cool slightly.

2 Whisk together the vinegar, mayonnaise, and mustard in a medium bowl and season with salt and pepper. Slowly whisk in the oil until emulsified. Fold in the crabmeat, green onions, and parsley until combined; season with salt and pepper.

3 Heat your grill to medium-high for direct grilling (see page 23).

4 Slice the potatoes in half lengthwise, brush the cut sides with oil, and season with salt, pepper, and a touch of cayenne. Put the potatoes on the grill, cut side down, and grill until lightly golden brown, about 2 minutes. Brush the tops with oil, flip over the potatoes, and continue grilling, covering the grill, until just cooked through, about 4 minutes longer.

5 Remove the potatoes to a platter and immediately spoon the crabmeat and green onion dressing over the halves.

At once easy and sophisticated, this potato salad is a play of contrasting flavors and textures. Naturally salty feta cheese plays up the brininess of olives, which in turn highlight the creamy potatoes and fresh, snappy green beans. I highly recommend that you parboil the potatoes before grilling them; they'll still pick up great grilled flavor and color, but the timing is so much easier to gauge. Always dress potato salads while the potatoes are still warm, so that they absorb the flavors of the dressing—in this case a tangy vinaigrette flecked with dill. **SERVES 4 TO 6**

15 fingerling potatoes
Kosher salt and freshly ground black
   pepper
½ pound haricots verts, trimmed
3 tablespoons red wine vinegar
1 tablespoon fresh lemon juice
2 teaspoons clover honey
½ cup extra-virgin olive oil
2 tablespoons finely chopped fresh dill
Canola oil
8 ounces feta cheese, crumbled
½ cup pitted kalamata olives
Fresh flat-leaf parsley leaves, for garnish

GRILLED FINGERLING POTATO SALAD ||| WITH ||| *feta, haricots verts,* ||| AND ||| *olives*

1 Put the potatoes in a large pot, cover with cold water by 2 inches, and add 2 tablespoons salt. Bring to a boil and cook until a small knife inserted into the center of a potato meets with some resistance, about 15 minutes. Scoop the potatoes out of the water, transfer to a baking sheet, and let cool slightly. Slice in half lengthwise.

2 Have ready a bowl of ice water. Add the haricots verts to the boiling water and cook until crisp-tender, about 3 to 4 minutes. Drain and transfer to the ice water to cool. Drain well.

3 Heat your grill to medium-high for direct grilling (see page 23).

4 Whisk together the vinegar, lemon juice, and honey in a large bowl; season with salt and pepper. Slowly whisk in the olive oil until emulsified. Whisk in the dill.

5 Brush the cut sides of the potatoes with canola oil and season with salt and pepper. Grill, cut side down, until lightly golden brown, about 2 minutes. Flip over the potatoes and continue grilling until just cooked through, about 2 minutes more.

6 Remove the potatoes to a platter and immediately drizzle with half of the vinaigrette. Add the green beans to the remaining vinaigrette in the bowl, season with salt and pepper, and toss to coat. Add to the potatoes on the platter and top with the feta, olives, and parsley leaves.

Literally translated, rajas means "strips," but in Mexican and Southwestern cooking, the term refers specifically to strips of roasted and peeled chiles. Mild yet peppery poblano chiles have the honors here. Thin-skinned new potatoes are fantastic on the grill; their slightly waxy texture holds up to the heat, taking on charred lines of flavor without falling apart. That said, like all potatoes, they do best when parboiled before they hit the grill. **SERVES 4 TO 6**

GRILLED NEW POTATOES

||| **WITH** ||| *queso fresco* ||| **AND** |||
grilled green rajas

3 poblano chiles
1 serrano chile
Canola oil
2 tablespoons red wine vinegar
2 tablespoons extra-virgin olive oil
2 tablespoons finely chopped fresh
    cilantro leaves, plus whole leaves for
    garnish
Kosher salt and freshly ground black
    pepper
2½ pounds new potatoes
8 ounces queso fresco, crumbled

1 Heat your grill to high for direct grilling (see page 23).

2 Brush the poblano and serrano chiles with canola oil and grill, turning as needed, until charred all over, about 10 minutes. Remove to a bowl, cover, and let sit for 10 minutes.

3 Turn your grill down to medium for direct grilling.

4 Peel and seed the chiles. Thinly slice the poblanos and finely chop the serrano. Combine the chiles, vinegar, olive oil, and chopped cilantro in a small bowl and season with salt and pepper. Let the rajas sit at room temperature for at least 30 minutes to allow the flavors to meld.

5 Meanwhile, put the potatoes in a pot, cover with cold water by 2 inches, and add 2 tablespoons salt. Bring to a boil over high heat and cook until a skewer inserted into the center of a potato meets some resistance, about 15 minutes. Drain well and let cool slightly.

6 Cut the potatoes in half, brush with canola oil, and season with salt and pepper. Grill cut side down until lightly golden brown, about 2 minutes. Turn the potatoes over, close the cover, and continue grilling until just cooked through, about 2 minutes.

7 Remove the potatoes to a platter, immediately sprinkle with the cheese, and top with the green chile rajas. Garnish with fresh cilantro leaves.

An abundance of mustard seeds grows in California's Napa Valley—as it does in the south of France; the regions share a similar climate. It makes sense, then, that many of the same ingredients feature prominently in both cuisines. These potatoes, grilled with a mustardy aioli (basically, garlic–scented mayonnaise) and served with a scattering of herbs, would be at home on either region's table. Delicate parsley, chives, and tarragon are known collectively as fines herbes and are a staple of Mediterranean cooking. **SERVES 4 TO 6**

½ cup mayonnaise

2 garlic cloves, smashed to a paste

1 heaping tablespoon Dijon mustard

1 heaping tablespoon whole grain mustard

Kosher salt and freshly ground black pepper

2½ pounds baby Yukon gold potatoes, scrubbed

2 tablespoons finely chopped fresh flat-leaf parsley leaves

1 tablespoon finely chopped fresh chives

1 tablespoon finely chopped fresh tarragon

MUSTARD AIOLI-GRILLED POTATOES ||| WITH ||| *fines herbes*

1 Whisk together the mayonnaise, garlic, and both mustards in a small bowl; season with salt and pepper. Cover the aioli and refrigerate for at least 30 minutes and up to 1 day.

2 Put the potatoes in a pot, cover with cold water by 2 inches, and add 2 tablespoons salt. Bring to a boil over high heat and cook until a skewer inserted into the center of a potato meets some resistance, 15 to 20 minutes. Drain well and let cool slightly.

3 Heat your grill to medium for direct grilling (see page 23).

4 Put the potatoes in a large bowl, toss with the aioli, and season with salt. Grill until golden brown on all sides, about 8 minutes.

5 Transfer the potatoes to a platter, sprinkle with the fresh herbs, and season with salt and pepper.

Potato salad is a classic American dish, and this version goes amazingly well with Texas-style barbecue. I love mustard, and this mustardy dressing pops with flavor and texture. Fire-roasted red peppers add a touch of smokiness and beautiful color. Using both the pickled onion and their pickling liquid in the dressing creates brightness that carries throughout the dish. Remember to mix in the dressing while the potatoes are still warm so that their open pores can absorb all that fantastic flavor. **SERVES 8**

1½ cups white wine vinegar
3 tablespoons sugar
1 teaspoon yellow mustard seeds
Kosher salt and freshly ground black pepper
1 small red onion, halved and thinly sliced
3 pounds new red potatoes
6 hard-boiled eggs, coarsely chopped
1 grilled or jarred roasted red bell pepper, peeled, seeded, and finely diced
1 cup mayonnaise
2 tablespoons Dijon mustard
2 tablespoons whole grain mustard
¼ cup fresh flat-leaf parsley or cilantro leaves

TEXAS-STYLE POTATO SALAD

||| **WITH** ||| *mustard* ||| **AND** |||

pickled red onion

1 Bring the vinegar, sugar, mustard seeds, and 1 tablespoon salt to a boil in a small saucepan and cook until the sugar and salt dissolve, about 1 minute. Transfer to a small bowl and let cool for 10 minutes. Add the onion and stir to combine. Cover and refrigerate for at least 1 hour and up to 24 hours.

2 Drain the onion into a bowl through a strainer; reserve the pickling liquid separately.

3 Put the potatoes in a large pot, cover with cold water by 2 inches, and add 2 tablespoons salt. Bring to a boil over high heat and cook until a knife inserted into the center of a potato meets with no resistance, 20 to 30 minutes, depending on the size. Drain the potatoes well, let cool slightly, and cut into ½-inch-thick slices.

4 Transfer the potatoes to a large bowl, add the eggs, pickled onions, and roasted pepper. Whisk together the mayonnaise, both mustards, a few tablespoons of the pickling liquid, 1 tablespoon salt, and ½ teaspoon black pepper. Add the dressing and parsley to the warm potatoes and gently mix to combine; season with salt and pepper. Serve at room temperature or cover tightly and refrigerate for at least 2 hours to serve chilled.

Rum and brown sugar are two favorite indulgences of mine and as both are made from sugarcane, they are a natural combination. Together they amp up the flavor of the naturally sweet potatoes. Smoke from the grill and spice from the rum balance the dish as much as the fresh citrusy hits of lime zest and lemony parsley.

SERVES 4 TO 6

BROWN SUGAR-RUM GRILLED SWEET POTATOES ||| WITH |||
lime zest ||| AND ||| *parsley*

4 sweet potatoes
Kosher salt and freshly ground black pepper
6 tablespoons (¾ stick) unsalted butter
¼ cup packed light brown sugar
¼ cup dark rum
¼ cup finely chopped fresh flat-leaf parsley leaves
Grated zest and juice of 1 lime
¼ cup canola oil

1 Put the sweet potatoes in a large pot, cover with cold water by 2 inches, and add 2 tablespoons salt. Bring to a boil and cook until a skewer or paring knife inserted into the center of a sweet potato meets with slight resistance, about 25 minutes. Drain well and let cool slightly. Cut each sweet potato into quarters.

2 Heat your grill to medium for direct grilling (see page 23).

3 Melt the butter in a small saucepan, add the brown sugar, and cook until smooth. Increase the heat, add the rum, and cook until reduced by half. Add the parsley, lime zest, and lime juice; season with salt and pepper.

4 Brush the sweet potatoes with oil and season with salt and pepper. Grill until golden brown on both sides, about 2 minutes. Brush with some of the rum glaze and grill for 1 minute longer.

5 Remove the sweet potatoes to a platter and brush with more of the glaze.

A truly satisfying salad, this dish can be served as a first course, but is just as appropriate as the star of a luncheon menu—and really, what could be better than a salad topped with sausage, egg, and cheese toast for brunch? For the chorizo, I like the D'Artagnan brand, which is a cross between soft and hard. Peppery arugula is a great foil for the rich and flavorful ingredients, and a mustardy vinaigrette finishes the dish with a bright, acidic touch. **SERVES 4**

1 (12-ounce) slice provolone cheese
(about 1½ inches thick)
1 pound chorizo
Canola oil
Kosher salt and freshly ground black
pepper
1 tablespoon finely chopped fresh
oregano
⅛ teaspoon red pepper flakes
Italian or French bread, cut into
¼-inch-thick slices
½ cup extra-virgin olive oil, plus more for
drizzling
2 tablespoons unsalted butter
4 large eggs
3 tablespoons aged sherry or red wine
vinegar
2 teaspoons Dijon mustard
1 teaspoon clover honey
4 ounces arugula
1 small red onion, halved and thinly
sliced
3 ripe tomatoes, cored and quartered
Chopped fresh chives, for garnish

TOMATO, RED ONION, AND ARUGULA SALAD
WITH *fried egg* AND *chorizo*

1 Two hours before grilling, remove the provolone from the refrigerator and let sit at room temperature. Letting the cheese sit out in the air will allow it to form a crust and will make it easier to grill.

2 Heat your grill to medium-high for direct and indirect grilling (see page 23).

3 Grill the chorizo, turning occasionally, until nicely charred and cooked through, about 15 minutes. Remove to a plate lined with paper towels. Let rest for 5 minutes and then roughly chop.

4 Heat a griddle on the grill over direct heat. Lightly brush the top of the provolone with canola oil and season with salt and pepper. Put on the griddle, seasoned side down, and cook until the cheese has a dark golden brown crust on the bottom, about 5 minutes. Brush the top lightly with canola oil, season with salt and pepper, and carefully flip over the cheese. Move the griddle over the cooler part of the grill (indirect heat), close the cover, and cook until lightly browned on the second side and melting. Remove to a plate and sprinkle with the oregano and red pepper flakes.

5 Grill the bread on each side until lightly golden brown, about 30 seconds per side. Remove to a platter, drizzle with olive oil, and season with salt and pepper. Spread the cheese onto the grilled bread.

6 Melt the butter in a cast-iron pan over medium heat. Crack the eggs into the pan, season with salt and pepper, and cook until the whites are set and the yolks are still runny, about 3 minutes.

7 While the eggs are cooking, whisk together the vinegar, mustard, and honey in a large bowl and season with salt and pepper. Slowly whisk in the olive oil until emulsified. Add the arugula, onion, and tomatoes and gently toss to coat.

8 Divide the salad, grilled bread, and chorizo among 4 large plates and top each with an egg. Garnish with chives.

Kale and radicchio both do quite well on the grill; the direct heat turns their edges charred and crispy while the inner leaves become tender and stay intact. Soaking the kale is important so that steam can build and cook the tough stalks as the leaves grill. Because kale and radicchio are both slightly bitter greens, they take to a sauerkraut-style dressing just as well as cabbage does. **SERVES 8**

½ cup plus 1 tablespoon canola oil,
    plus more for brushing
1 large shallot, chopped
½ cup apple cider vinegar
8 juniper berries
½ teaspoon caraway seeds
½ teaspoon yellow mustard seeds
3 fresh thyme sprigs
1 to 2 tablespoons sugar, to taste
Kosher salt and freshly ground black
    pepper
3 heads radicchio, halved lengthwise
2 big bunches kale, soaked in cold water

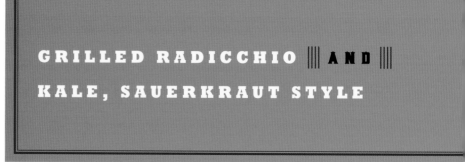

GRILLED RADICCHIO ||| AND |||
KALE, SAUERKRAUT STYLE

1 Heat 1 tablespoon of the oil in a small saucepan over medium heat. Add the shallot and cook until soft, about 2 minutes. Add the vinegar, juniper berries, caraway seeds, mustard seeds, thyme, sugar, 1 teaspoon salt, and ¼ teaspoon pepper. Bring to a boil and cook until the sugar and salt are dissolved, 1 to 2 minutes. Remove from the heat. Let sit for 15 minutes then strain into a small bowl, discarding the solids. Slowly whisk in the remaining ½ cup oil until emulsified.

2 Heat your grill to high for direct grilling (see page 23).

3 Brush the cut sides of the radicchio with oil and season with salt and pepper. Grill, cut side down, until golden brown and slightly charred, 2 to 3 minutes. Brush the tops with oil, flip over the radicchio, and continue grilling until just heated through, 2 to 3 minutes longer. Remove from the grill. Thinly slice the radicchio and put it in a bowl.

4 Remove the kale from the water and shake gently to get some of the water off. Season with salt and pepper and place on the grill. Cook until slightly wilted and charred on all sides, about 30 seconds per side. Remove from the grill. Thinly slice and add to the radicchio.

5 Add the dressing to the radicchio and kale and toss to coat. Let sit at room temperature for 30 minutes to allow the flavors to meld.

Caribbean food is so much more than just rice and beans, and yet . . . the region is known for the dish for a reason. The comforting basic, made with creamy coconut milk, is given new life as a salad when mixed with this herbaceous and savory pesto.

SERVES 4 TO 6

1 cup unsweetened coconut milk
2 cups long-grain rice
Kosher salt and freshly ground black
    pepper
1 cup packed fresh cilantro leaves
1 cup packed fresh basil leaves
1 garlic clove, chopped
¼ cup walnuts
½ cup extra-virgin olive oil
¼ cup freshly grated Parmesan cheese
1 (15-ounce) can black-eyed peas,
    drained, rinsed, and drained again

BLACK-EYED PEAS ‖ AND ‖ RICE
‖ WITH ‖ *cilantro-basil pesto*

1 Bring 2¾ cups water and the coconut milk to a boil in a medium saucepan. Add the rice, 2 teaspoons salt, and ¼ teaspoon pepper and return to a boil. Cover, reduce the heat to medium-low, and cook until the liquid is absorbed and the rice is tender, about 18 minutes. Remove from the heat, cover, and let sit for 5 minutes.

2 Combine the cilantro, basil, garlic, and walnuts in a food processor and process until coarsely chopped; season with salt and pepper. With the motor running, add the oil and process until emulsified. Add the Parmesan and salt and pepper to taste and pulse a few times to incorporate. (The pesto can be made up to 1 day in advance and stored, tightly covered, in the refrigerator.)

3 Fluff the rice with a fork, transfer to a bowl, and add the black-eyed peas. Add ¼ cup cold water to the pesto and mix to combine. Add the pesto to the rice, season with salt and pepper, and toss to combine. Serve warm or at room temperature.

Sweet and smoky baked beans are a classic accompaniment to barbecue. What makes these particular beans better than anything you could pour out of a can? That would be the burnt ends, which is another way to describe the trimmings from smoked brisket. These tough, chewy, incredibly flavorful pieces of meat are tenderized as they cook by the liquid in the beans and flavor the whole dish with their intense smokiness. **SERVES 8**

HONEY-RUM BAKED BLACK BEANS
||| **WITH** ||| *burnt ends*

End pieces from Smoked Spice-Rubbed Brisket, Texas Style (page 174)
3 tablespoons canola oil
2 cups Bobby Flay's Mesa Barbecue Sauce (see Sources) or your favorite barbecue sauce
½ pound double-smoked slab bacon, cut into small dice
1 medium Spanish onion, cut into small dice
1 medium carrot, cut into small dice
4 garlic cloves, finely chopped
2 (15-ounce) cans pinto beans, drained, rinsed well, and drained again
¼ cup clover honey
3 tablespoons packed light brown sugar
2 cups low-sodium chicken broth
¼ cup plus 2 tablespoons coarsely chopped fresh flat-leaf parsley leaves
Kosher salt and freshly ground black pepper

1 Heat your grill to medium-high for indirect grilling (see page 23).

2 Brush the brisket on both sides with 2 tablespoons of the oil and grill, basting with 1 cup of the barbecue sauce every few minutes, until slightly charred and crisp, about 15 minutes. Remove from the grill and let rest for 10 minutes. Cut the brisket into small dice and reserve 2 cups for the beans.

3 Heat the remaining 1 tablespoon oil in a medium cast-iron or enamel-coated cast-iron Dutch oven over medium heat. Add the bacon and cook until crisp, about 10 minutes. Remove with a slotted spoon to a plate lined with paper towels.

4 Add the onion and carrot to the bacon fat in the pan and cook until soft, about 5 minutes. Add the garlic and cook for 1 minute. Add the beans, honey, brown sugar, chicken broth, the remaining 1 cup barbecue sauce, and ¼ cup of the parsley and mix gently to combine; season with salt and pepper.

5 Cover the pan and set on the grill over indirect heat. Cover the grill and bake for 20 minutes. Check to see if the mixture is dry; if it is, add a little more broth and continue baking for another 20 minutes. Remove the lid and bake the beans until golden brown on top, another 15 minutes.

6 Garnish the top with the remaining 2 tablespoons parsley and let sit for 10 minutes. Fold in the burnt ends just before serving.

Similar to a Spanish red rice, this seasoned, tomatoey rice dish is a South Carolinian specialty. Typically served hot, it can be a somewhat heavy side dish in its traditional form. But cooled down with a bright, herbaceous vinaigrette of sweet mint and paired with tender stalks of grilled asparagus, this rice dish is at once altogether lighter than the original and yet satisfying enough, especially with those crisp salty bits of bacon, to be served as a main course for lunch. **SERVES 4 TO 6**

TOMATO RED RICE ||| WITH |||
grilled asparagus
||| AND ||| sweet mint dressing

¼ cup fresh mint leaves, finely chopped, plus more leaves for garnish
½ cup rice vinegar
¼ cup clover honey
Kosher salt and freshly ground black pepper
⅓ cup plus 5 tablespoons canola oil
6 plum tomatoes
8 ounces slab bacon, cut into small dice
1 small Spanish onion, finely diced
2 cups long-grain rice
12 asparagus spears, trimmed

1 Heat your grill to high for direct grilling (see page 23).

2 Combine the mint, rice vinegar, and honey in a bowl and season with salt and pepper. Whisk in ⅓ cup of the oil until emulsified.

3 Brush the tomatoes with 2 tablespoons of the remaining oil and season with salt and pepper. Grill the tomatoes until charred on all sides and very soft, about 6 minutes.

4 Remove the tomatoes from the grill, halve them, and remove the seeds. Put the tomatoes in a blender and blend until smooth. Transfer to a measuring cup and add enough cold water to make 4 cups liquid.

5 Heat 1 tablespoon of the remaining oil in a medium saucepan over medium heat. Add the bacon and cook until the bacon is crisp and the fat has rendered, about 10 minutes. Remove with a slotted spoon to a plate lined with paper towels. Add the onion to the pan and cook until soft, about 4 minutes. Add the rice and cook, stirring constantly, for 1 minute. Stir in the tomato mixture, 2 teaspoons salt, and ¼ teaspoon pepper. Bring to a boil and reduce the heat to medium-low. Cover and cook until the rice is tender and the liquid has been absorbed, about 18 minutes. Remove from the heat and let sit, covered, for 5 minutes.

6 While the rice is cooking, brush the asparagus with the remaining 2 tablespoons oil and season with salt and pepper. Grill until just cooked through, about 1½ minutes per side. Remove from the grill, put a plate, and toss with a few tablespoons of the mint dressing.

7 Fluff the rice with a fork and transfer to a platter. Top with the asparagus and drizzle with more of the dressing. Tear some mint leaves over the top. Serve warm or at room temperature.

Pickled peaches, perfectly plump pink shrimp . . . it's Georgia's best! This refreshing ceviche hits all those great flavor notes—at once sweet, spicy, tangy, and fresh. Using the pickling liquid from the peaches as part of the bath for the shrimp really helps unify the dish's two main ingredients. **SERVES 4 TO 6**

Kosher salt and freshly ground black pepper
1 pound (21 to 24 count) shrimp, shelled and deveined
5 large radishes, cut into thin matchsticks
½ English cucumber, cut into small dice
2 halves Quick Pickled Peaches (recipe follows), thinly sliced, plus 1½ cups peach pickling liquid
¼ cup pickled Vidalia onions (see below), drained
Grated zest and juice of 1 lime
¼ cup fresh flat-leaf parsley leaves
¼ cup celery leaves

GULF SHRIMP ||| AND ||| SPICY PICKLED PEACH CEVICHE

1 Bring 4 cups salted water to a boil in a medium saucepan. Add the shrimp and cook for 1 minute. Drain, rinse with cold water, and drain again. Slice each shrimp in half lengthwise and put in a large nonreactive bowl.

2 Add the radishes, cucumber, pickled peaches, peach liquid, onions, lime zest, lime juice, and parsley to the bowl and season with salt and pepper. Cover and refrigerate for 30 minutes.

3 Use a slotted spoon to divide the ceviche among bowls. Garnish with the celery leaves.

QUICK PICKLED PEACHES
MAKES 8 PEACH HALVES

4 just slightly underripe peaches
1 small Vidalia onion, halved and thinly sliced
2 cups rice vinegar
1½ cups sugar
1 (2-inch) piece fresh ginger, peeled and sliced
2 teaspoons kosher salt
½ teaspoon allspice berries
½ teaspoon coriander seeds
½ teaspoon black peppercorns
½ teaspoon yellow mustard seeds
½ teaspoon red pepper flakes

1. Fill a large pot with water and bring to a boil. Have ready a bowl with ice water. Cut a small X on the top and bottom of each peach. Boil the peaches for 30 seconds. Remove with a slotted spoon and immediately transfer to the ice water. Reserve 2 cups of the boiling water. Once cool, drain the peaches, then halve and pit them. Put in a 2-quart Mason jar with the onion.
2. In a large nonreactive saucepan, boil the reserved 2 cups water, the rice vinegar, sugar, ginger, salt, allspice, coriander seeds, peppercorns, mustard seeds, and red pepper flakes until the sugar is completely dissolved, about 5 minutes. Remove from the heat and cool to room temperature.
3. Pour the cooled vinegar mixture over the peaches, cover, and refrigerate for at least 8 hours and up to 48 hours.

Perfect for hot summer days, this ceviche is cool and refreshing—not to mention healthful. As delicious as this dish is, it is just as beautiful to look at with its deep red tomatoes, juicy cubes of orange mango, bright pink pickled onions, and varying shades of green from cilantro, green onions, and a serrano chile. Just a note: Because the grouper and shrimp are "cooked" by the acid of the lime juice and not with heat, it is vital that they be absolutely fresh. **SERVES 4 TO 6**

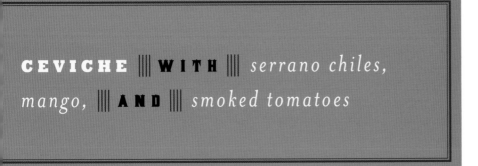

CEVICHE ||| WITH ||| serrano chiles, mango, ||| AND ||| smoked tomatoes

1 Soak 1 cup of cherry or mesquite wood chips for 30 minutes.

2 Heat your grill to very low for indirect grilling (see page 23).

3 If using a charcoal grill, scatter the drained wood chips over the coals. If the temperature in the grill is hotter than 100°F, put 2 cups ice cubes in an aluminum tray and nestle the tray next to the coals on the bottom grate. Put the cooking grate in place. If using a gas grill, put the drained wood chips in a smoker box. Add the tray of ice cubes, if needed, to the cooking grate. Then, for either grill, close the cover and let smoke build until the temperature in the grill reaches 100°F.

4 Brush the tomatoes with oil, season with salt and pepper, and arrange in a single layer in a grill basket or on a baking sheet. Transfer to the grill, close the cover, and cold-smoke the tomatoes for 10 to 20 minutes, depending upon how smoky you want them.

5 Combine the grouper and shrimp in a nonreactive bowl. Add the lime zest and lime juice, cover, and refrigerate for 20 minutes.

6 Using a slotted spoon, transfer the seafood to a clean bowl; discard the marinade. Add the tomatoes, mango, green onions, red onions, serrano, chopped cilantro, hot sauce, orange zest, and orange juice. Season with salt and pepper and toss gently to combine. Let sit for 5 minutes.

7 Use a slotted spoon to divide the ceviche among bowls. Serve with the plantain chips and garnish with cilantro leaves.

1 pint grape tomatoes
Canola oil
Kosher salt and freshly ground black pepper
12 ounces fresh grouper, cut into small dice
1 pound large (21 to 24 count) shrimp, shelled, deveined, and halved
Grated zest of 1 lime
2 cups fresh lime juice
1 small ripe mango, halved, pitted, and finely diced
2 green onions, green and pale green parts, thinly sliced
¼ cup pickled red onions and their juice (page 98)
1 serrano chile, finely diced
¼ cup finely chopped fresh cilantro leaves, plus whole leaves for garnish
2 teaspoons Scotch bonnet hot sauce
1 teaspoon grated orange zest
2 cups fresh orange juice
Plantain chips

POULTI

This recipe calls for a whole lot of rosemary, and it is all put to good use. Every morsel of the bird is infused with the piney, fragrant freshness of rosemary. Half of the sprigs are paired with garlic, peppercorns, and mellow honey in a brine that pumps the chicken with flavor and moisture. The other half joins the wood in your smoker, creating a rosemary-scented smoke that infuses the chicken with even more succulent flavor. The secret to a crisp-skinned bird is to remove it from its brine, pat dry with paper towels, and store unwrapped in the refrigerator for at least an hour before cooking so that the skin can dry. **SERVES 4**

TUSCAN ROSEMARY-SMOKED WHOLE CHICKEN

2 cups low-sodium chicken broth
½ cup kosher salt
¼ cup clover honey
2 teaspoons black peppercorns
8 garlic cloves, smashed
20 large fresh rosemary sprigs
1 (4-pound) chicken, excess fat trimmed
¼ cup canola oil
Freshly ground black pepper

1 To make the brine, pour 6 cups cold water and the chicken broth into a large saucepan. Add the salt, honey, peppercorns, garlic, and 12 of the rosemary sprigs and bring to a boil, stirring to dissolve the salt. Remove from the heat, let cool to room temperature, and then refrigerate until completely chilled.

2 At least 3½ hours before you plan to smoke your chicken, pour the brine mixture into a large clean container. Add the chicken, breast side down. Cover and refrigerate for 2 to 4 hours.

3 Remove the chicken from the brine, rinse well with cold water, and pat dry with paper towels. Put the chicken skin side up on a baking rack set over a baking sheet, and refrigerate for at least 1 hour and up to 4 hours. This will allow the skin to dry out and produce a crisper skin while cooking.

4 Soak 2 cups wood chips, preferably almond (cherry or apple will also work nicely), and the remaining 8 rosemary sprigs in water for at least 30 minutes. Remove the chicken from the refrigerator 30 minutes before cooking.

5 Heat your smoker according to the manufacturer's instructions. If using a charcoal or gas grill, set up a drip pan with water on the bottom grates and heat the grill to low for indirect grilling (see page 23). For a charcoal grill, put half of the drained wood chips and rosemary sprigs over the hot coals, add the cooking grate, and close the cover. For a gas grill, add the drained wood chips and rosemary to a smoker box or foil pouch, put on the cooking grates of the grill toward the back, and close the cover. For both grills, open the vents halfway and maintain a temperature between 275°F and 325°F. Let smoke build for 10 minutes.

6 Brush the chicken with oil and season all over with ground black pepper. Put the chicken in the smoker or grill over the pan filled with water. Smoke for 45 minutes. Add the remaining drained wood chips and rosemary sprigs, add more water if needed to the drip pan—and hot coals if needed—and continue to smoke the chicken until an instant-read thermometer inserted into a breast (not touching a bone) registers 160°F and a thigh reaches 170°F, about 45 minutes more, depending on the size of the chicken.

7 Remove the chicken from the grill, tent loosely with foil, and let rest for 10 minutes before carving.

This fragrant and spicy jerk marinade gives an instant shot of Jamaican flavor to smoky wings. Pimento wood, which comes from the allspice tree, provides the unique smoke flavor of authentic Jamaican jerk chicken. Hard to find in the United States, the wood really has no exact substitute, but apple and pecan wood are your closest bets. Stay away from stronger woods, such as hickory or mesquite, which will overpower the flavor of the jerk marinade. Tart tamarind concentrate (which you can find in Middle Eastern stores and online; see Sources) combines with mellow honey to make a mouthwatering glaze. These wings are destined to become a tailgating classic. **SERVES 4**

¼ cup kosher salt, plus more for
　　seasoning
¼ cup sugar
1 head garlic, sliced crosswise
1 bunch fresh thyme sprigs
4 cinnamon sticks
2 teaspoons allspice berries
2 teaspoons black peppercorns
1 Scotch bonnet chile, with a small slit
　　made in the side
3 pounds chicken wings
¼ cup canola oil
Spicy Honey-Tamarind Glaze (recipe
　　follows)
Chopped green onion, for garnish

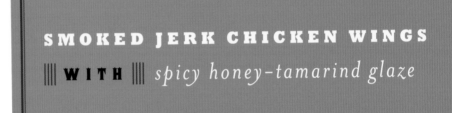

SMOKED JERK CHICKEN WINGS
WITH *spicy honey-tamarind glaze*

1 Combine 2 quarts water, the salt, and sugar in a medium saucepan, bring to a boil, and cook until the salt and sugar dissolve, about 5 minutes. Remove from the heat and add the garlic, thyme, cinnamon, allspice, peppercorns, and Scotch bonnet. Let the brine cool completely.

2 Add the chicken wings to the brine, cover, and refrigerate for at least 4 hours and up to 8 hours.

3 Remove the wings from the brine, rinse well with cold water, and pat dry. Put the wings on a baking rack set over a baking sheet and put in the refrigerator to dry for at least 1 hour and up to 8 hours.

4 Soak 2 cups pimento or apple wood chips in water for at least 30 minutes.

5 Heat your grill to medium for indirect grilling (see page 23).

6 Add the drained wood chips to the coals in a charcoal grill or put them in a smoker box of a gas grill. Close the grill cover and let smoke build for 10 minutes.

7 Add the wings to the grill directly over the heat source, close the lid, and grill until golden brown on both sides, about 10 minutes per side. Transfer to the cooler side of the grill (indirect heat), cover the grill, and continue cooking until the wings are cooked through, about 15 minutes.

8 Put the chicken wings in a large bowl. Add the honey-tamarind glaze and toss to coat. Season with salt, transfer to a platter, and garnish with green onion.

SPICY HONEY-TAMARIND GLAZE

MAKES ABOUT 1½ CUPS

2 tablespoons canola oil
1 (2-inch) piece fresh ginger, peeled and finely grated
¾ cup fresh orange juice
3 tablespoons tamarind concentrate
¼ cup ketchup
¼ cup clover honey
1 tablespoon red wine vinegar
2 teaspoons Sriracha or spicy chile paste
Kosher salt and freshly ground black pepper

Heat the oil in a small saucepan over medium-high heat. Add the ginger and cook until soft, about 2 minutes. Pour in the orange juice and ½ cup water and bring to a simmer. Add the tamarind, ketchup, and honey and cook, stirring occasionally, for 5 minutes. Remove from the heat, whisk in the vinegar and Sriracha, and season with salt and pepper. Let cool slightly.

A buttermilk bath does wonders for grilled chicken, too—it's not fair to leave all its tenderizing, flavor-boosting goodness to fried chicken alone. Do be sure to take the chicken out of the chile-spiked brine at least an hour and a half before heading out to the grill. Giving the exterior a chance to dry out helps to ensure a super-crisp skin. The sweet yet spicy honey glaze is a great fruity touch to balance the earthiness of the chiles in the marinade. **SERVES 4**

1 quart buttermilk
2 tablespoons ancho chile powder
1 tablespoon New Mexican chile powder
1 tablespoon cascabel chile powder
½ teaspoon chile de árbol powder or cayenne
1 teaspoon smoked mild paprika
1 teaspoon ground coriander
1 teaspoon granulated garlic
1 teaspoon onion powder
½ teaspoon ground cinnamon
4 (8-ounce) bone-in, skin-on chicken breast halves
4 chicken drumsticks
¼ cup canola oil
Kosher salt and freshly ground black pepper
Mango-Honey Glaze (recipe follows)

GRILLED RED CHILE-BUTTERMILK BRINED CHICKEN
WITH *spicy mango-honey glaze*

1 Whisk together the buttermilk, chile powders, paprika, coriander, garlic, granulated onion powder, and cinnamon in a large baking dish. Add the chicken and turn to coat. Cover and refrigerate for at least 4 hours and up to 24 hours, turning a few more times.

2 Remove the chicken from the brine and pat dry with paper towels. Put the chicken on a baking rack set over a baking sheet. Return to the refrigerator and let sit, uncovered, for at least 1 hour and up to 4 hours.

3 Heat your grill to medium for indirect grilling (see page 23). Remove the chicken from the refrigerator 30 minutes before cooking.

4 Brush the chicken on both sides with the oil and season with salt and pepper.

Put the chicken, skin side down, on the hotter side of the grill (direct heat) and grill until browned, 4 to 5 minutes. Turn over the chicken and continue grilling until the bottom is golden brown, 4 to 5 minutes. Move to the cooler side of the grill (indirect heat), close the cover, and continue grilling until an instant-read thermometer inserted into the thickest part of the breast (not touching the bone) registers 160°F, about 10 minutes longer. During the last few minutes, brush with some of the mango-honey glaze.

5 Remove the chicken to a platter and drizzle with more of the glaze. Tent loosely with foil and let rest for 10 minutes before serving.

MANGO-HONEY GLAZE

MAKES ABOUT 1½ CUPS

2 tablespoons canola oil
1 small Spanish onion, chopped
1 garlic clove, chopped
3 large very ripe mangoes, peeled, pitted,
    and chopped
½ cup dry white wine
¼ cup pineapple juice
¼ cup fresh orange juice
¼ to ½ teaspoon chile de árbol powder,
    to taste
3 tablespoons clover honey
Kosher salt and freshly ground black
    pepper

1. Heat the oil in a large high-sided sauté
pan over medium-high heat. Add the onion
and cook until soft, about 4 minutes. Add
the garlic and cook for 1 minute. Add the
mangoes and cook, stirring occasionally,
until broken down and caramelized, about
10 minutes. Add the white wine and cook
until reduced by half, about 2 minutes.
2. Carefully transfer the mixture to a
blender, add the pineapple and orange
juices and the chile de árbol powder and
blend until smooth, about 2 minutes.
Strain into a bowl and season with the
honey and salt and pepper. The mixture
should be a thick puree. If it is too thick,
thin it with a touch of water. Let cool to
room temperature before serving.

Think chicken paillard, northern California style. The concept remains the same—a simply prepared, thinly pounded chicken breast topped with a cool salad—but the execution is something else. A mix of plump grapes, crunchy almonds, and charred Fresno chiles is mounted on sweet and tangy apricot-glazed chicken before the whole thing is dressed with a grainy mustard vinaigrette for a dish that just pops with flavor. Keeping with the California wine country theme, I call for Chardonnay vinegar in the dressing; it lends a delicate buttery flavor that I love. **SERVES 4**

GRILLED APRICOT-GLAZED CHICKEN SALAD ||| WITH ||| *almonds* ||| AND ||| *fresno chiles*

1 teaspoon yellow mustard seeds

½ cup Chardonnay or other white wine vinegar

1 tablespoon finely diced shallot

2 teaspoons Dijon mustard

1 teaspoon clover honey

Kosher salt and freshly ground black pepper

¼ cup plus 1 tablespoon extra-virgin olive oil

3 Fresno chiles

Canola oil

1 cup seedless red grapes, halved

1 cup green grapes, halved

½ cup sliced almonds, lightly toasted

1 tablespoon finely chopped fresh chives

¾ cup apricot jam

4 (6-ounce) boneless, skinless chicken breast halves, thinly pounded

1 Heat the mustard seeds in a small sauté pan over low heat until they pop and become fragrant, about 2 minutes. Remove to bowl, whisk in 5 tablespoons of the vinegar, the shallot, mustard, and honey; season with salt and pepper. Slowly add ¼ cup of the olive oil and whisk until emulsified.

2 Heat your grill to high for direct grilling (see page 23).

3 Brush the Fresno chiles with canola oil and grill, turning as needed, until charred all over, about 10 minutes. Remove to a bowl, cover, and let sit for 10 minutes. Peel, seed, and then thinly slice the chiles.

4 Combine the chiles, red and green grapes, almonds, and chives in a bowl and toss with the remaining 1 tablespoon olive oil.

5 Whisk together the apricot jam and the remaining 3 tablespoons vinegar and season with salt and pepper. Brush the chicken on both sides with canola oil and season with salt and pepper. Grill, brushing with some of the glaze, until golden brown on both sides and just cooked through, about 2½ minutes per side.

6 Remove each piece of chicken to a large dinner plate. Top with the grape salad and drizzle with the vinaigrette.

Crispy skinned and oh so juicy, this smoked chicken is loaded with flavor. The pungent paste of fruity ginger, lime zest, tons of garlic, and nutty black mustard seeds would be more than enough to ensure a tasty chicken, but this dish takes everything one step further. Cardamom pods, whole sticks of cinnamon, and cloves added to the charcoal in the smoker or grill create a fragrant environment—it's like culinary incense—wherein the spices fully permeate the chicken. Sumac is a deep red spice with a tart flavor that is classically paired with onions in Indian and Middle Eastern cooking; this relish adds a fresh bite to the heady smoked chicken. **SERVES 4**

SMOKED GINGER CHICKEN ||| WITH |||
cardamom, cloves, ||| AND ||| cinnamon

2 tablespoons canola oil

1 (4-inch) piece fresh ginger, peeled and coarsely chopped

1 head garlic, cloves separated and peeled

1 teaspoon black mustard seeds

Grated zest of 2 limes

Kosher salt and freshly ground black pepper

1 (3-pound) chicken, butterflied and lightly pounded for even thickness

10 cardamom pods

5 cinnamon sticks

1 tablespoon whole cloves

1 medium red onion, halved and thinly sliced

3 tablespoons finely chopped fresh flat-leaf parsley leaves

½ teaspoon sumac

Kosher salt and freshly ground black pepper

1 Heat the oil in a medium sauté pan over medium heat, add the ginger and garlic cloves, and cook until soft, about 2 minutes. Add the mustard seeds and cook for 30 seconds. Add ½ cup water and the lime zest and season with salt and pepper. Bring to a boil and cook for 1 minute. Transfer the mixture to a blender and blend to a smooth paste, adding more water if needed. Let cool.

2 Rub the paste over the entire chicken, including under the skin. Cover and marinate in the refrigerator for at least 2 hours and up to 8 hours. Remove the chicken from the refrigerator 30 minutes before cooking.

3 Combine the cardamom, cinnamon, and cloves in a bowl. Cover with cold water and soak for at least 1 hour and up to 4 hours.

4 Combine the red onion and 1 tablespoon salt in a bowl and let sit at room temperature for 30 minutes. Rinse with cold water and drain well. Put the onion in a bowl and add the parsley and sumac.

5 Heat your grill to high for indirect grilling (see page 23).

6 Drain the spices and add them evenly over the hot coals in a charcoal grill or to a smoker box of a gas grill. Put the lid on the grill and allow smoke to fill the grill, about 10 minutes.

7 Season the chicken on both sides with salt and pepper. Put the chicken, skin side down, on the cooler side of the grill (indirect heat), close the cover, and grill until the skin is lightly golden brown with faint grill marks, 22 to 25 minutes. Turn the chicken skin side up, move to the hot side of the grill (direct heat), and continue grilling until the skin is golden brown, 12 to 15 minutes. Flip the chicken once more and continue grilling over direct heat until the skin is golden brown and crisp and an instant-read thermometer inserted into the thigh registers 165°F, about 8 minutes.

8 Remove the chicken to a cutting board, tent loosely with foil, and let rest for 10 minutes before carving. Top the chicken with some of the onion–parsley relish.

In its day, Charleston, South Carolina, was a hub of the spice trade, and its residents adopted curries, such as the spice mixture in this rub, as their own. At this point, curry is practically as authentically southern as pecan pie! Sorghum—you can think of it as the South's maple syrup—is sweet yet earthy with a touch of spice that a dash of chile de árbol brings to the forefront. If you can't find sorghum, a combination of honey and molasses will do the trick. **SERVES 4 TO 6**

½ cup plus 2 teaspoons kosher salt
¼ cup sugar
12 bone-in, skin-on chicken thighs
3 tablespoons ancho chile powder, plus
 more for garnish
2 teaspoons ground cumin
2 teaspoons ground coriander
2 teaspoons ground fennel
2 teaspoons ground turmeric
1 teaspoon ground cardamom
1 teaspoon ground cloves
1 teaspoon freshly ground black pepper
⅛ teaspoon chile de árbol powder
¼ cup canola oil
Sorghum-Chile Glaze (recipe follows)

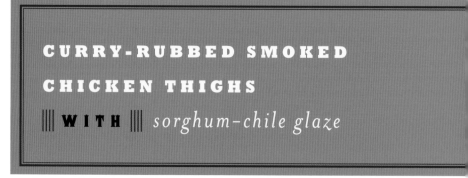

CURRY-RUBBED SMOKED CHICKEN THIGHS
||| WITH ||| *sorghum-chile glaze*

1 To make the brine, bring 4 cups cold water, ½ cup of the salt, and the sugar to a boil in a medium saucepan and cook until the salt and sugar are dissolved, about 2 minutes. Remove from the heat and let cool completely.

2 Put the chicken thighs in a bowl, add the cooled brine, cover, and refrigerate for 30 minutes and up to 1 hour. Remove from the brine, rinse well, and pat dry with paper towels.

3 Combine all the spices with the remaining 2 teaspoons salt in a small bowl. Rub each chicken thigh with some of the spice rub, put in a zip-top bag, and refrigerate for at least 1 hour and up to 8 hours.

4 Soak 1 cup apple or hickory wood chips in water for at least 30 minutes. Remove the chicken from the refrigerator 30 minutes before cooking.

5 Heat your smoker according to the manufacturer's instructions. If using a charcoal or gas grill, set up a drip pan with water on the bottom grates and heat the grill to low for indirect grilling (see page 23). For a charcoal grill, put half of the drained wood chips over the hot coals, add the cooking grate, and close the cover. For a gas grill, add the wood chips to a smoker box or foil pouch, put on the cooking grates of the grill toward the back, and close the cover. For both grills, open the vents halfway and maintain a temperature around 250°F. Let smoke build for 10 minutes.

6 Put the chicken in the smoker or grill over the pan filled with water. Smoke for 40 minutes. Add the remaining drained wood chips, add more water if needed to the drip pan—and hot coals if needed—and continue to smoke the chicken until an instant-read thermometer inserted into a thigh registered 165°F, about 1 hour more. During the last 15 minutes of smoking, brush the thighs with some of the glaze.

7 Remove the chicken from the grill, tent loosely with foil, and let rest for 10 minutes. Serve brushed with more of the glaze and sprinkled with ancho powder.

SORGHUM-CHILE GLAZE
MAKES ¾ CUP

¾ cup sorghum
1 teaspoon chile de árbol powder
Kosher salt and freshly ground
    black pepper

Whisk together the sorghum and
chile de árbol powder; season with
salt and pepper. Cover and let sit
at room temperature for at least
30 minutes before serving.

This juicy chicken literally translates as "devil's chicken" in Italian, and a quick glance at the recipe—full of garlic, black pepper, and chile de árbol—will tell you why. There's a great continuity of flavors here as the essential elements of the brine are carried through in a fiery chile oil that both bastes and infuses the chicken with a blast of flavor. Crisp, slightly sweet, and bright with zesty lemon, fennel slaw finishes the dish on a refreshing note. **SERVES 4**

1 cup kosher salt
1 teaspoon black peppercorns
8 dried chiles de árbol, crushed
1 head garlic, halved lengthwise
1 (3-pound) chicken, butterflied
Chile Oil (recipe follows)
Lemony Fennel Slaw (recipe follows)
Lemon wedges
Fresh flat-leaf parsley leaves, for garnish

BRINED BUTTERFLIED CHICKEN ALLA DIAVOLO
||| **WITH** ||| *lemony fennel slaw*

1 Combine 2 quarts cold water, the salt, peppercorns, chiles de árbol, and garlic in a large saucepan. Bring to a boil and cook until the salt dissolves, 5 minutes. Remove from the heat and let the brine cool completely.

2 Add the chicken to the brine, cover, and refrigerate for at least 1 hour and up to 4 hours.

3 Remove the chicken from the brine, rinse well with cold water, and pat dry with paper towels. Place the chicken on a baking rack set over a baking sheet and put, skin side up, in the refrigerator for at least 1 hour and up to 4 hours. This will allow the skin to dry out and produce a crisper crust on the grill.

4 Heat your grill to medium-high for indirect grilling (see page 23). Remove the chicken from the refrigerator 30 minutes before cooking.

5 Brush the entire chicken with 3 table-spoons of the chile oil. Put, skin side down, on the cooler side of the grill (indirect heat), close the cover, and grill until the skin is lightly golden brown with faint grill marks, 22 to 25 minutes. Turn the chicken skin side up, move to the hot side of the grill (direct heat), and continue grilling until the skin is golden brown, 12 to 15 minutes. Flip the chicken once more and continue grilling over direct heat until the skin is golden brown and crisp and an instant-read thermometer

inserted into the thigh registers 165°F, about 8 minutes.

6 Remove the chicken to a cutting board, tent loosely with foil, and let rest for 10 minutes before carving. Carve the chicken and drizzle with more chile oil. Serve with the fennel slaw, lemon wedges, and a sprinkle of parsley leaves.

CHILE OIL
MAKES 1 CUP

1 cup canola oil
6 dried chiles de árbol, lightly toasted
    and crushed
8 black peppercorns
6 garlic cloves, chopped
1 teaspoon kosher salt
1 teaspoon fresh oregano leaves

Combine the oil, chiles de árbol, pepper-corns, garlic, salt, and oregano in a small saucepan and bring to a simmer over low heat. Remove from the heat and let sit at room temperature for at least 30 minutes and up to 4 hours. Transfer to a blender and blend until smooth. Strain into a bowl.

LEMONY FENNEL SLAW
SERVES 4 TO 6

⅔ cup mayonnaise
1 teaspoon grated lemon zest
¼ cup fresh lemon juice
2 tablespoons extra-virgin olive oil
2 tablespoons sugar
1 large fennel bulb, thinly sliced,
    plus ¼ cup fennel fronds
1 small head Savoy cabbage, thinly sliced
½ cup fresh flat-leaf parsley leaves
Kosher salt and freshly ground black pepper

Whisk together the mayonnaise, lemon zest, lemon juice, oil, and sugar in a large bowl. Add the sliced fennel, fennel fronds, cabbage, and parsley and season with salt and pepper. Cover and refrigerate for at least 30 minutes.

One of the many things I love about living in New York City is its vast array of casual international restaurants. I didn't have to go far to be introduced to this Peruvian dish of super-flavorful rotisserie chicken and its accompanying green garlic–chile sauce. Tangy, slightly spicy aji verde sauce will become your new go-to sauce when you need a punch of flavor. Peruvians serve it as a dipping sauce for bread, but I think it's at home with eggs, potatoes, tortilla or plantain chips, and of course served alongside this moist and savory chicken. Traditionally this chicken is cooked on a rotisserie; if you don't have one, butterfly the chicken and cook as for Brined Butterflied Chicken alla Diavolo (page 126). **SERVES 4**

3 tablespoons canola oil
8 garlic cloves, chopped
1 tablespoon ground cumin
1 tablespoon mild Spanish paprika
1 tablespoon ancho chile powder
¼ cup white wine vinegar
3 tablespoons low-sodium soy sauce
Juice of 1 lemon
Kosher salt and freshly ground black pepper
1 (3½- to 4-pound) chicken, rinsed well and patted dry
Aji Verde Sauce (recipe follows)
¼ cup crumbled cotija cheese

PERUVIAN CHICKEN
||| WITH ||| *aji verde sauce*

1 Heat the oil in a medium sauté pan over medium heat. Add the garlic and cook until soft, 1 minute. Add the cumin, paprika, and ancho powder and cook for 30 seconds. Add ¼ cup water, the vinegar, and soy sauce and cook, stirring constantly, for 30 seconds. Transfer to a blender, add the lemon juice, and season with salt and pepper. Blend to a paste, adding a little more water if needed. Let cool to room temperature.

2 Rub the entire chicken (under the skin and in the cavity, too) with the mixture. Put in a large bowl or baking dish, cover, and let marinate in the refrigerator for at least 4 hours and up to 24 hours.

3 Remove the chicken from the refrigerator 30 minutes before cooking. Soak a little butcher's twine in water for 10 minutes and then use it to tie the legs closed.

4 Prepare the rotisserie on your grill according to the manufacturer's directions and heat to medium-high heat.

5 Skewer the chicken from tail to neck on the rotisserie spit. Slide the second prong onto the spit and make sure the chicken is held snugly in place. Attach the spit to the rotisserie.

6 Reduce the heat to medium. Activate the turning mechanism and grill the chicken until golden brown all over and an instant-read thermometer inserted into the thickest part of the thigh registers 165°F, about 1½ hours at 350°F.

7 Remove the chicken from the rotisserie, tent loosely with foil, and let rest for 10 minutes before carving. Serve with the aji verde sauce and a sprinkling of cotija cheese.

AJI VERDE SAUCE
MAKES ABOUT 1 CUP

½ cup packed fresh cilantro leaves
¼ cup packed fresh mint leaves
1 serrano chile, chopped
1 garlic clove, chopped
1 tablespoon white wine vinegar
1 teaspoon clover honey
½ cup extra-virgin olive oil
¼ cup grated cotija cheese
Kosher salt and freshly ground black pepper

Combine the cilantro, mint, serrano, garlic,
¼ cup water, the vinegar, and honey in a
blender and blend until smooth. With the
motor running, slowly add the olive oil and
blend until emulsified. Transfer to a bowl,
stir in the cheese, and season with salt and
pepper.

This succulent, mahogany-skinned chicken has humble roots; the dish originated in roadside stands in Mexico's Sinaloa region and is truly street food. Or at least it was . . . Juicy yet crisp, at once earthy and acidic, this chicken deserves a spot on your table, too. Serve it with this healthful relish of hearty black beans, toothsome quinoa, sweet charred corn, and the dish's traditional accompaniment, green onions. **SERVES 4 TO 6**

½ cup rice vinegar
Juice of 1 orange
Juice of 1 lime
8 garlic cloves, coarsely chopped
3 tablespoons ancho chile powder
1 tablespoon mild Spanish paprika
1 teaspoon ground cinnamon
½ teaspoon ground cloves
½ teaspoon ground allspice
½ teaspoon chile de árbol powder or
   cayenne
¼ cup canola oil
2 (3-pound) chickens, each cut into
   8 pieces
Kosher salt and freshly ground black
   pepper
Grilled Corn, Black Bean, and Quinoa
   Relish (recipe follows)

MEXICAN RED CHICKEN ||| WITH ||| *grilled corn, black bean,* ||| AND ||| *quinoa relish*

1 Whisk together the rice vinegar, orange and lime juices, garlic, ancho powder, paprika, cinnamon, cloves, allspice, chile de árbol powder, and oil in a bowl. Put the chicken pieces in a large baking dish; pour the marinade over and rub into each piece of chicken very well. Cover and refrigerate for at least 4 hours and up to 8 hours.

2 Soak 2 cups apple or mesquite wood chips in water for at least 30 minutes.

3 Heat your grill to medium for indirect grilling (see page 23). Remove the chicken from the refrigerator 30 minutes before cooking.

4 Remove the chicken from the marinade and pat dry with paper towels. Season the chicken on both sides with salt and pepper. Put the chicken, skin side down, on the hotter side of the grill (direct heat) and grill until browned, 4 to 5 minutes. Turn over the chicken and continue grilling until the bottom is golden brown, 4 to 5 minutes. Move to the cooler side of the grill (indirect heat), close the cover, and continue grilling until an instant-read thermometer inserted into the thickest part of the breast (not touching the bone) registers 160°F, about 10 minutes longer.

5 Remove the chicken to a platter, tent loosely with foil, and let rest for 10 minutes before serving. Serve with the corn, black bean, and quinoa relish.

GRILLED CORN, BLACK BEAN, AND QUINOA RELISH

SERVES 4 TO 6

Kosher salt and freshly ground black pepper
1 cup quinoa
8 ears of corn
6 green onions
2 tablespoons canola oil
1 (15.5-ounce) can black beans, drained, rinsed well,
    and drained again
Juice of 1 lime
¼ cup extra-virgin olive oil

1. Heat your grill to high for direct grilling (see page 23).
2. Bring 2 cups water to a boil, add 1 teaspoon salt and ¼ teaspoon pepper, and stir in the quinoa. Cover and cook over medium heat until the quinoa is tender and the water is absorbed, about 15 minutes. Remove from the heat and let sit, covered, for 5 minutes.
3. Pull the outer husks down each ear of corn to the base. Strip away the silk from each ear of corn. Fold the husks back into place and tie the ends together with kitchen string. Place the ears of corn in a large bowl of cold water with 1 tablespoon salt for 10 minutes.
4. Remove the corn from the water and shake off the excess. Put on the grill, close the cover, and grill, turning every 2 minutes, for 10 minutes, or until the kernels are almost tender when pierced with a paring knife. Set aside to cool at least slightly and then cut the kernels from the cobs.
5. Brush the green onions with the canola oil and season with salt and pepper. Grill the onions until soft and slightly charred, about 2 minutes per side. Remove and coarsely chop.
6. Fluff the quinoa with a fork and transfer to a large bowl. Stir in the corn, green onions, black beans, lime juice, and olive oil and season with salt and pepper. Let the relish sit at room temperature for at least 30 minutes before serving to allow the flavors to meld.

This super-easy, lemony chicken is a family favorite of my wife's, a Texas girl through and through. When Stephanie was young, her mother, Laura, recently divorced and happy to have an easy fix in the dinner rotation, made it for her two daughters all the time. Laura was channeling a recipe she remembered her father making for her when she was a little girl. To this day, the smell of this dish cooking instantly transports Stephanie back to her childhood. For two generations, the ingredients and the taste have remained exactly the same. The only change I have made is to upgrade the bottled steak sauce in the marinade to a homemade version. (And yes, it goes amazingly well with steak, too.) **SERVES 6 TO 8**

Juice of 2 lemons
1 cup Steak Sauce (recipe follows)
1 tablespoon Worcestershire sauce
2 (3-pound) chickens, butterflied
8 tablespoons (1 stick) unsalted butter,
    at room temperature
Kosher salt and freshly ground black
    pepper

DADDY'S GRILLED CHICKEN

STEAK SAUCE
MAKES ABOUT 2 CUPS

2 tablespoons canola oil
½ small Spanish onion, grated
1 garlic clove, finely chopped
½ cup dark raisins
1 cup ketchup
¼ cup fresh lemon juice
¼ cup white wine vinegar
3 tablespoons Worcestershire sauce
2 tablespoons low-sodium soy sauce
2 teaspoons Dijon mustard

1 Whisk together the lemon juice, steak sauce, and Worcestershire in a small bowl. Put the chickens in a large baking dish, rub them with the butter, and then pour the lemon mixture over them. Cover and refrigerate for at least 2 hours and up to 4 hours.

2 Heat your grill to medium-high for indirect grilling (see page 23). Remove the chickens from the refrigerator 30 minutes before cooking.

3 Season the chicken on both sides with salt and pepper. Put the chicken, skin side down, on the cooler side of the grill (indirect heat), close the cover, and grill until the skin is lightly golden brown with faint grill marks, 22 to 25 minutes. Turn the chicken skin side up, move to the hot side of the grill (direct heat), and continue grilling until the skin is golden brown, 12 to 15 minutes. Flip the chicken once more and continue grilling over direct heat until the skin is golden brown and crisp and an instant-read thermometer inserted into the thigh registers 165°F, about 8 minutes.

4 Remove the chicken to a cutting board, tent loosely with foil, and let rest for 10 minutes before carving.

Heat the oil in a medium saucepan over medium-high heat. Add the onion and cook until soft, about 4 minutes. Add the garlic and cook for 30 seconds. Add the raisins and ½ cup water and boil until the water has evaporated, about 5 minutes. Add the ketchup, lemon juice, vinegar, Worcestershire, and soy sauce and cook, stirring occasionally, until thickened and the flavors have melded, about 20 minutes. Remove from the heat and let cool completely. (The sauce can be made up to 2 days in advance and stored, covered, in the refrigerator.)

Brazil's version of chicken salad, chicken salpicao is packed with flavor and crunch and is a fantastic summer dish. Though the salad is typically made with roasted or poached chicken, grilling the lean chicken breasts before shredding them adds another dimension of slightly charred flavor, echoed by the grilled red onions. Classically— and some might say imperatively—this dish is topped with fried shoestring potatoes, but I like the slight variation of vegetable chip sticks, which give the same salty crunch but with a touch more flavor and certainly more color. **SERVES 4 TO 6**

4 ears of corn
Kosher salt and freshly ground black
    pepper
3 (8-ounce) boneless, skinless chicken
    breast halves
2 medium red onions, cut into ¼-inch-
    thick rings
Canola oil
3 carrots, shredded
½ cup thinly sliced green onions, white
    and green parts
¼ cup chopped fresh flat-leaf parsley
    leaves
2 cups mayonnaise
¼ cup low-sodium chicken broth
2 tablespoons aged sherry or red wine
    vinegar
3 garlic cloves, smashed and chopped to
    a paste
1½ tablespoons smoked mild Spanish
    paprika
1 (7.5-ounce) bag high-quality vegetable
    chip sticks, such as Terra

GRILLED CHICKEN SALPICAO

1 Heat your grill to high for direct grilling (see page 23).

2 Pull the outer husks down each ear of corn to the base. Strip away the silk from each ear of corn. Fold the husks back into place and tie the ends together with kitchen string. Place the ears of corn in a large bowl of cold water with 1 tablespoon salt for 10 minutes.

3 Remove the corn from the water and shake off the excess. Put the corn on the grill, close the cover, and grill, turning every 5 minutes, for 15 to 20 minutes, or until the kernels are tender when pierced with a paring knife. When cool enough to handle, cut the kernels from the cobs and put in a large bowl.

4 Brush the chicken and red onions on both sides with oil and season with salt and pepper. Grill the chicken for 5 minutes on each side or until slightly charred and just cooked through. Remove to a plate, tent loosely with foil, and let rest for 5 minutes before shredding into thin pieces. Transfer to the bowl with the corn.

5 Grill the red onions until slightly charred and just cooked through, 3 to 4 minutes per side. Add to the chicken along with the carrots, green onions, and parsley.

6 Whisk together the mayonnaise, chicken broth, vinegar, garlic, paprika, and salt and pepper to taste in a bowl until smooth. Pour the mayonnaise mixture over the chicken and gently toss to coat. Transfer the chicken to a platter, top with vegetable chip sticks, and serve.

Lean turkey breast is a great changeup from everyday chicken breasts, especially when prepared with this anything-but-everyday spice rub. Slightly sweet with a smoky heat, the rub also creates an unbelievable crust on the exterior of the turkey. Incredibly moist from its brining and smoking, this turkey breast would be perfect for a smaller Thanksgiving celebration. **SERVES 4 TO 6**

APPLE WOOD-SMOKED BRINED TURKEY BREAST
||| **WITH** ||| *chile-cinnamon rub*

½ cup kosher salt
½ cup granulated sugar
1 (3- to 4-pound) boneless turkey breast
¼ cup ancho chile powder
2 tablespoons packed light brown sugar
1 tablespoon ground cumin
2 teaspoons ground cinnamon
¼ teaspoon freshly ground black pepper
Canola oil

1 To make the brine, bring 2 quarts cold water to a boil. Add the salt and granulated sugar and cook until dissolved, about 2 minutes. Pour into a large container with a lid and let cool completely.

2 Add the turkey breast to the cooled brine, cover, and refrigerate for 45 minutes.

3 Remove the turkey from the brine, rinse well, and pat dry with paper towels. Put the turkey on a plate and return to the refrigerator, uncovered, for at least 1 hour and up to 4 hours.

4 To make the rub, stir together the ancho powder, brown sugar, cumin, cinnamon, and pepper in a small bowl.

5 Soak 1 cup apple wood chips in water for at least 30 minutes.

6 Heat your grill to medium-high for indirect grilling (see page 23). Remove the turkey from the refrigerator 30 minutes before smoking.

7 Add the drained wood chips to the coals in a charcoal grill or put them in a smoker box of a gas grill. Close the cover and let smoke build for 10 minutes.

8 Brush the turkey with oil and rub the skin side of the turkey with the rub. Put the turkey on the grill directly over the heat source, rubbed side down, and grill until slightly charred and a crust has formed,

about 5 minutes. Turn over the turkey, move it to the cooler part of the grill (indirect heat), close the cover, and continue cooking for 30 to 40 minutes, or until an instant-read thermometer inserted into the center of the breast registers 155°F.

9 Remove the turkey from the heat, tent loosely with foil, and let rest for 10 minutes before slicing.

Thanksgiving is my favorite holiday, by far. It's a great day to spend cooking and then celebrating with friends and family. I'll sometimes have upward of forty people at my house when it's all said and done! I am up at 4 a.m. to get my first turkey started, and with that much effort, I want to serve something that doesn't taste like everyone else's. Perfectly moist and seasoned inside and out, there is nothing humdrum about this bird. Make this in a Big Green Egg or in a Caja China—it's great either way. **SERVES 4 TO 6**

6 tablespoons mild Spanish paprika
2½ tablespoons New Mexican chile powder
1 teaspoon chile de árbol powder
¼ teaspoon cayenne
4 teaspoons garlic powder
4 teaspoons onion powder
4 teaspoons dried thyme
4 teaspoons dried oregano
1½ cups kosher salt
¼ cup packed light brown sugar
2 fresh bay leaves (not dried)
1 large Spanish onion, quartered
4 garlic cloves
1 (12-pound) fresh turkey
Nonstick cooking spray
¼ cup canola oil

CAJUN BRINED TURKEY, TWO WAYS

1 To make the rub, combine the paprika, chile powders, cayenne, garlic and onion powders, thyme, and oregano in a small bowl.

2 Combine 2 gallons cold water, the salt, and brown sugar in a large (at least 16-quart) stockpot. Bring to a boil and cook to dissolve the salt and sugar, 5 minutes. Remove from the heat and whisk in half of the spice rub, the bay leaves, onion, and garlic. Let cool completely.

3 Add the turkey to the brine, cover, and refrigerate or set in a very cold place (between 32°F and 40°F) for at least 12 hours and up to 24 hours.

4 Remove the turkey from the brine 1 hour before cooking. Rinse well under cold water and pat dry with paper towels.

5 Soak 3 cups hickory or apple wood chips in water for at least 30 minutes.

6 Heat a smoker or charcoal grill to medium for indirect grilling (see page 23). A Big Green Egg is perfect to use here, if you have one. Add half of the drained wood chips to the coals, close the cover, and let smoke build for 10 minutes.

7 Spray a V-shape rack liberally with nonstick cooking spray. Brush the turkey with oil and rub the entire turkey (including the cavity) with the remaining spice rub. Put the turkey on the rack, breast side down. Place the turkey and rack over the cooler part of the grill (indirect heat). Open the grill cover vents halfway and close the cover, positioning the vents over the turkey. Cook for 1 hour at 350°F.

8 Uncover the grill and, using very thick potholders, transfer the V rack and turkey to a rimmed baking sheet or roasting pan. Remove the grill cooking grate, replenish the charcoal, and add the remaining drained wood chips. Replace the grate. Carefully flip the turkey, breast side up, in the rack. Return the rack and turkey to the cooler part of the grill (indirect heat). Cover and cook for 45 minutes. Insert an instant-read thermometer into each thigh to check the temperature and gauge how much longer the turkey needs to cook (the thigh should register 165°F). A 12-pound turkey should take 2 hours to 2¼ hours total to cook.

9 Remove the turkey from the grill, tent loosely with foil, and let rest for 30 minutes before carving.

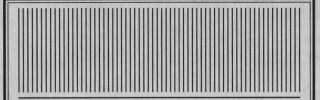

CAJA CHINA METHOD

1 Follow steps 1 to 4, opposite.

2 Prepare your Caja China for cooking according to the manufacturer's directions. Light 12 pounds of charcoal for model #1 or 16 pounds for model #2 in batches in a chimney starter and allow to burn until covered with a fine layer of gray ash, 20 to 25 minutes.

3 Brush the turkey with the canola oil and rub all over with the rub. Put the turkey on the rack of the Caja China, breast side down. Cover the box with the ash pan and charcoal grid. Spread the hot charcoal over the grid. Cook for 30 minutes. Flip over the turkey so that it is breast side up and cook, adding hot charcoal as needed according to the manufacturer's directions, until an instant-read thermometer inserted into the thigh registers 165°F, about 1 hour more.

4 Remove the turkey from the box, tent loosely with foil, and let rest for 20 minutes before carving.

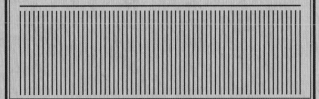

Paella might be the most well known of Spain's national dishes. Layered with chicken, chorizo sausage, and shellfish and studded with peas and chile peppers, it's such a beautiful, bountiful dish—an impressive one for company. When we would make this at my Spanish–Mediterranean restaurant, Bolo, diners would wonder how we got the rice to be so luxurious, and I am sharing my secret with you here: It's the last-minute addition of a garlicky mayonnaise that coats each grain of rice. I prefer to cook the many elements of my paella separately and then bring them together in the final dish so that I can be sure that each component is cooked properly; this method translates especially well to the grill. **SERVES 6 TO 8**

PAELLA ON THE GRILL

2 (2-pound) live lobsters

1 (3-pound) chicken, cut into 8 pieces

1 cup canola oil

Kosher salt and freshly ground black pepper

1 pound Spanish chorizo (cross between hard and soft) from D'Artagnan, see Sources

12 colossal (U-15 or U-10) shrimp, tails on, peeled, and deveined

12 sea scallops, patted dry

6 plum tomatoes, halved

4 lemons, halved

8 cups low-sodium chicken broth

Large pinch of saffron

1 large Spanish onion, chopped

6 garlic cloves, finely chopped

2 cups short-grain rice

1 pound clams, soaked in water and scrubbed

1 pound mussels, bearded and scrubbed

1 (15.5-ounce) can chickpeas, drained, rinsed well, and drained again

1 cup frozen peas, thawed

6 jarred piquillo peppers, thinly sliced

½ cup mayonnaise

1 cup chopped fresh flat-leaf parsley leaves

1 Bring a large pot of salted water to a boil. Add the lobsters, cover the pot, and cook for 12 minutes. Remove the lobsters, drain well, and then halve lengthwise with a sharp knife.

2 Heat your grill to high for indirect grilling (see page 23).

3 Brush the chicken with some of the oil and season with salt and pepper. Put the chicken, skin side down, on the cooler part of the grill (indirect heat), close the cover, and cook the chicken until golden brown and the skin is crisp, about 10 minutes. Flip over the chicken and continue grilling until almost completely cooked through, 8 to 10 minutes for breasts and about 10 minutes for thighs. (The chicken will finish cooking in the rice.) Remove to a baking sheet.

4 Brush the chorizo, lobsters, shrimp, scallops, tomatoes, and lemons with some of the oil and season with salt and pepper on both sides. Grill the chorizo until charred and just cooked through, about 10 minutes. Let cool slightly and then cut into ½-inch slices. Grill the lobster, cut side down, until charred and just cooked through, about 5 minutes. Remove the tail meat from the shell and cut into pieces; remove the claw meat from the shell, too. Grill the shrimp and scallops until slightly charred and almost cooked through, about 1 minute per side. Grill the tomatoes, cut side down, until slightly charred, about 1½ minutes. Flip over the tomatoes and

continue grilling for another minute. Grill the lemons, cut side down, until charred, about 45 seconds. Remove all the ingredients to baking sheets as they cook.

5 Combine the chicken broth and saffron in a large saucepan and bring to a simmer. Heat 3 tablespoons of the canola oil in a large paella pan. Add the onion and cook until soft, about 5 minutes. Add 4 of the garlic cloves and cook for 1 minute. Add the rice and cook, stirring constantly, for a few minutes. Begin adding the broth, 1 cup or so at a time, and cook, stirring constantly, until the rice is al dente, about 25 minutes.

6 Arrange the chicken in the rice and cook for 5 minutes. Add the clams, mussels, shrimp, scallops, chorizo, tomatoes, chickpeas, peas, and piquillo peppers, and cook until the clams and mussels open, about 8 minutes. Discard any clams or mussels that don't open. Add the lobster meat.

7 Whisk together the mayonnaise, the remaining 2 garlic cloves, and the juice of half of a grilled lemon in a large bowl until combined. Add the rice mixture and toss to coat. Stir in the parsley and season with salt and pepper. Serve garnished with the remaining grilled lemon halves.

With high levels of acidity and sugar, tamarind has a sweet-and-sour fruity flavor that pairs beautifully with duck. Tamarind concentrate, also known as tamarind paste, is widely used in Southeast Asian cuisine as well as Latin and Mexican dishes, so look for it in both areas of your local markets; it's also readily available online. Pineapple, caramelized on the grill, joins tangy, habanero-heated pickled onions in a delicious, colorful relish. This is a showstopper of a dish. **SERVES 4 TO 6**

PINEAPPLE RELISH

Kosher salt and freshly ground black
   pepper
1 tablespoon sugar
1 cup fresh lime juice
½ cup distilled white vinegar
½ small habanero chile
1 large red onion, halved and cut into
   ⅛-inch-thick slices
½ teaspoon dried Mexican oregano
½ golden pineapple, cored and cut into
   ¼-inch-thick slices
Canola oil
2 large green onions, green and pale
   green parts, thinly sliced
¼ cup chopped fresh cilantro leaves

DUCK

8 dried guajillo chiles, stemmed
½ cup tamarind concentrate
½ cup clover honey
¼ cup fresh lime juice
8 garlic cloves, roasted
½ cup lightly packed fresh cilantro
   leaves
2 tablespoons fresh mint leaves
Kosher salt and freshly ground black
   pepper
5 (8-ounce) Magret duck breast halves,
   trimmed of excess fat
12 (6-inch) corn tortillas

TAMARIND-GLAZED DUCK TACOS
||| **WITH** ||| *grilled pineapple-onion relish*

1 **Make the pineapple relish:** Put 1 tablespoon salt, the sugar, lime juice, vinegar, and habanero in a small nonreactive saucepan. Bring to a boil and cook until the sugar and salt are dissolved, about 2 minutes. Let cool for 5 minutes.

2 Combine the red onion and oregano in a medium nonreactive bowl. Add the vinegar mixture and stir to combine. Top with a small plate to weight down the mixture slightly, cover with plastic wrap, and refrigerate for at least 4 hours and up to 24 hours.

3 Heat your grill to high for indirect grilling (see page 23).

4 **Meanwhile, start to prepare the duck:** Soak the guajillos in boiling water for 30 minutes to soften.

5 Meanwhile, brush the pineapple with oil and season with salt and pepper. Grill directly over the heat source until charred on both sides and just cooked through, about 2 minutes per side. Remove to a cutting board, cut into small dice, and transfer to a bowl. Add some of the pickled red onions and the brining liquid, the green onions, and chopped cilantro and season with salt and pepper. Let sit at room temperature for 30 minutes before serving. Keep the grill on.

6 Combine the guajillos, ½ cup of the soaking liquid, the tamarind, honey, lime juice, and garlic in a saucepan, bring to a simmer, and cook for 15 minutes. Remove from the heat and let cool for 10 minutes. Transfer to a food processor, add the cilantro leaves and mint, and season with salt and pepper. Process until smooth, then pour the glaze into a bowl and let cool.

7 Have ready a squeeze bottle filled with water to handle flare-ups. Score the duck breasts with a sharp knife to make a diagonal crosshatch pattern and season liberally with salt and pepper. Put the duck, skin side down, on the cooler part of the grill (indirect heat) and cook, uncovered, until the skin is nicely browned, about 10 minutes. Turn over the breasts and continue grilling until medium-rare (140°F on an instant-read thermometer), about 4 minutes longer, brushing with the glaze during the last few minutes of grilling. Remove the breasts to a cutting board and brush with more of the glaze. Tent loosely with foil and let rest for 5 minutes.

8 Slice the duck on the diagonal into ¼-inch-thick slices. Grill the tortillas for about 10 seconds per side over direct heat. Fill the tortillas with duck slices and some pineapple relish.

PORK

Cuban food is not to be confused with other types of Latin cuisine—it's not spicy and what it lacks in heat, it more than makes up for with herbaceous, garlicky, citrus-punched flavor. The marinade for this pork butt is simple, but it makes an impact as it becomes one with the meat. Cooked slowly in a Caja China, the pork will be perfect every time because the fat melts into the meat and leaves it fork-tender. The tropical guava glaze, added only in the last hour of cooking so that the sugars don't burn, turns into an irresistible lacquer. A fresh and crunchy slaw balances the rich pulled pork in this insanely good sandwich. **SERVES 8**

OPEN-FACED CUBAN PULLED PORK SANDWICHES

||| **WITH** ||| *sour orange-jicama slaw*

1 Using a paring knife, make small slits over the entire surface of the pork and rub the chopped garlic into the slashes.

2 Combine the oil and oregano leaves in a blender and blend until smooth. Put the pork in a large roasting pan or bowl, add the oregano marinade, and turn to coat. Cover and refrigerate for at least 8 hours and up to 24 hours.

3 Remove the pork from the marinade and pat dry with paper towels. Let sit at room temperature for 1 hour.

4 Whisk together the guava jelly, mustard, orange zest, and orange juice in a bowl and season with salt and pepper.

5 Prepare your Caja China according to the manufacturer's directions. Light 12 pounds of charcoal for model #1 or 16 pounds for model #2 in batches in a chimney starter and allow to burn until covered with a fine layer of gray ash, 20 to 25 minutes.

6 Season the pork liberally with salt and pepper. Put the pork on the rack of the Caja China. Cover the box with the ash pan

1 (4-pound) pork butt

5 garlic cloves, finely chopped, plus 3 cloves, smashed to a paste

¾ cup canola oil

Scant ¼ cup fresh oregano leaves, plus 2 teaspoons finely chopped

1½ cups guava jelly

¼ cup Dijon mustard

Finely grated zest of 1 orange

¼ cup fresh orange juice

Kosher salt and freshly ground black pepper

8 tablespoons (1 stick) unsalted butter, softened

4 Cuban bread loaves or foot-long soft baguettes, sliced lengthwise

½ cup mayonnaise

Sour Orange-Jicama Slaw (recipe follows)

recipe continues >>

and charcoal grid. Spread the hot charcoal over the grid. Cook, adding hot charcoal as needed, according to the manufacturer's directions, for 2½ hours.

7 After 2½ hours, baste with the guava glaze and continue to cook, basting every 15 minutes, until an instant-read thermometer inserted into the center of the roast registers 180°F, about 1 hour more.

8 Remove the roast from the box, tent loosely with foil, and let rest for 20 minutes. Using tongs, pull the pork into bite-sized pieces and toss with more of the guava glaze.

9 Stir together the butter, garlic paste, and chopped oregano and season with salt and pepper. Spread each half of bread with some of the garlic butter and place on a hot grill pan until lightly golden brown, about 20 seconds.

10 Spread both sides of the bread with some of the mayonnaise. Mound some of the pork on top of the mayonnaise and top the pork with some of the slaw. Serve the sandwiches open faced.

SOUR ORANGE-JICAMA SLAW
SERVES 8

1 teaspoon grated orange zest
½ teaspoon grated lime zest
½ cup fresh orange juice
¼ cup fresh lime juice
1 tablespoon sugar
1 small red onion, halved and thinly sliced
½ jicama, julienned
¼ head red cabbage, finely shredded
1 large carrot, julienned
3 tablespoons chopped fresh cilantro leaves
Kosher salt and freshly ground black pepper

Whisk together the orange and lime zests and juices and the sugar in a large bowl. Add the onion, jicama, cabbage, carrot, and cilantro and season with salt and pepper. Cover and refrigerate for at least 1 hour before serving to allow the flavors to meld.

Slightly sweet and smoky, Spanish paprika is made for barbecue. Its strengths are played up in both the sauce, tangy with Spanish sherry vinegar, and the spice-heavy rub. Rack of pork is lean with very little fat; a long briny soak ensures moist and flavorful—never dry—pork. **SERVES 6 TO 8**

GRILLED RACK OF PORK, TWO WAYS

½ cup plus 4 teaspoons kosher salt
½ cup packed light brown sugar
1 Spanish onion, quartered
15 black peppercorns
15 whole yellow mustard seeds
1 small bunch fresh thyme sprigs
1 (4-pound) center-cut rack of pork
¼ cup mild Spanish paprika
4 teaspoons ground cumin
4 teaspoons mustard powder
4 teaspoons ground fennel
2 teaspoons coarsely ground black pepper
Canola oil
Sherry Vinegar Barbecue Sauce (recipe follows)

1 To make the brine, combine 2½ quarts cold water, ½ cup of the salt, the brown sugar, onion, peppercorns, whole mustard seeds, and thyme in a pot large enough to hold the rack of pork and bring to a boil, whisking to dissolve the salt and sugar. Remove from the heat and let cool completely.

2 Add the pork to the brine, cover, and refrigerate for at least 4 hours and up to 12 hours.

3 Remove the pork from the brine 1 hour before cooking, rinse with cold water, and pat dry with paper towels.

4 Heat your grill to high for indirect grilling (see page 23).

5 Combine the paprika, cumin, mustard powder, fennel, ground pepper, and the remaining 4 teaspoons salt in a bowl. Brush the rack of pork with oil and rub with the spices and salt. Sear the pork on both sides directly over high heat until lightly golden brown and a crust has formed, about 5 minutes per side. Move the pork to the cooler side of the grill (indirect heat), close the cover, and cook, brushing with the barbecue sauce every 5 minutes or so, until an instant-read thermometer inserted into the center registers 140°F, about 30 minutes.

6 Remove the pork from the grill, tent loosely with foil, and let rest for 15 minutes before slicing.

recipe continues >>

SHERRY VINEGAR BARBECUE SAUCE

MAKES ABOUT 2 CUPS

2 tablespoons canola oil
2 shallots, finely diced
4 garlic cloves, finely chopped
1 cup aged sherry vinegar
¼ cup packed dark brown sugar
1 tablespoon mild Spanish paprika
1 cup ketchup
1 cup low-sodium chicken broth
2 teaspoons finely chopped fresh thyme
Kosher salt and freshly ground black pepper
Clover honey

Heat the oil in a medium saucepan over medium-high heat. Add the shallots and garlic and cook until softened, 1 minute. Add the vinegar and cook until reduced by half, about 5 minutes. Add the brown sugar, paprika, ketchup, chicken broth, and thyme and cook until reduced by half, about 15 minutes. Season with salt, pepper, and honey to taste. Let cool to room temperature.

SPANISH "CUBAN" SANDWICHES

COOK ON PLANCHA OR FLATTOP GRILL

SERVES 2

½ cup mayonnaise
2 garlic cloves, chopped
1 heaping tablespoon Dijon mustard
2 jarred piquillo peppers
Kosher salt and freshly ground black pepper
2 Cuban rolls or loaf of Cuban bread
¼ pound thinly sliced Manchego cheese
¼ pound thinly sliced Serrano ham
1 pound thinly sliced cooked rack of pork (from previous page)
2 cups baby arugula
4 tablespoons (½ stick) softened unsalted butter

1 Combine the mayonnaise, garlic, mustard, and piquillo peppers in a food processor and process until smooth; season with salt and pepper.

2 Heat a plancha or a cast-iron griddle over medium heat.

3 Spread both sides of each roll with some of the garlic mayonnaise. Layer the tops with a few slices of Manchego and then the ham. Top the bottom halves with some of the pork and the arugula. Put the tops on the sandwich, brush the tops with some of the butter, and put the sandwiches on the griddle, butter side down. Place a foil-wrapped brick on top and cook until the bread is crisp, about 3 minutes. Remove the brick, brush with more butter, flip over the sandwiches, and place the brick back on top. Continue cooking until the bottoms are crisp and the cheese is melted. Serve hot.

Pork shoulder is a cut that was made for smoking. Cooking it low and slow over indirect heat transforms the sinewy meat into fork-tender, insanely flavorful stuff. Because of the long smoking time, this recipe is meant for a smoker or a charcoal (not gas) grill. An adobo marinade with its acidic citrus juices further tenderizes the pork, while a heady mix of ground spices boosts flavor. Delicate, feathery Napa cabbage slaw is a fresh ending, its crunch a nice contrast to the smoked pork. A sprinkle of queso fresco adds just a touch of salty tang; if you can't find queso fresco, mild feta cheese is an easy substitute. **SERVES 8**

3 tablespoons canola oil
6 garlic cloves, chopped
4 teaspoons ground cumin
4 teaspoons ground coriander
½ cup ancho chile powder
4 canned chipotles in adobo, finely
    chopped
Grated zest of 2 oranges
1 cup fresh orange juice
Grated zest of 4 limes
½ cup fresh lime juice
6 tablespoons packed light brown sugar
2 tablespoons chopped fresh thyme
1 (5-pound) boneless pork shoulder
Kosher salt and freshly ground black
    pepper
1 dozen soft hamburger buns
Napa Slaw (recipe follows)
Dill pickle slices or sour pickles

SLOW-SMOKED PORK SHOULDER
WITH *napa slaw* AND *queso fresco*

1 Heat the oil in a small saucepan over medium heat. Add the garlic and cook until soft, about 1 minute. Add the cumin, coriander, and ancho powder and cook for 1 minute. Add 1 cup water and cook for 2 minutes. Add the chipotles, orange zest, orange juice, lime zest, lime juice, brown sugar, and thyme and cook until the brown sugar is dissolved, 2 minutes. Remove from the heat and let cool. (The adobo sauce can be made ahead and stored, covered, in the refrigerator for up to 2 days.)

2 Put the pork in a large plastic zip-top bag, add half of the adobo sauce, and refrigerate for at least 8 hours and up to 24 hours.

3 Remove the pork from the refrigerator 1 hour before cooking and pat dry with paper towels. Discard the marinade.

4 Soak 2 cups hickory or apple wood chips in water for at least 30 minutes. Divide the remaining adobo sauce in half: one half for basting and one half for serving.

5 Heat your smoker according to the manufacturer's instructions. If using a charcoal grill, set up a drip pan with water on the bottom grates and heat the grill to low for indirect grilling (see page 23). Put half of the drained wood chips over the hot coals, add the cooking grate, and close the cover. Open the vents halfway and maintain a temperature between 225°F and 250°F. Let smoke build for 10 minutes.

6 Season the pork with salt and pepper. Add the pork to the smoker or grill over the pan filled with water and close the cover. Smoke, turning over the pork and brushing it with some of the sauce every 45 minutes, until it reaches an internal temperature of 180°F. This can take about 6 hours. Adjust the heat as needed to maintain the temperature, add drained wood chips and hot coals as needed, and add more water to the drip pan if needed.

7 Remove the pork from the grill, tent loosely with foil, and let rest for 20 minutes. Using tongs, pull the pork into bite-sized pieces.

8 Mound the pork on a platter, pouring any accumulated juices over the meat. Toss with some of the reserved sauce and mound on buns with Napa Slaw and pickles, if desired.

NAPA SLAW
SERVES 8

2 cups coarsely chopped green onions, white and green parts
½ cup apple cider vinegar
4 serrano chiles
¼ cup mayonnaise
4 teaspoons sugar or clover honey
½ cup canola oil
Kosher salt and freshly ground black pepper
½ cup chopped fresh cilantro leaves
2 heads Napa cabbage, finely shredded
2 large carrots, julienned
2 small red onions, halved and thinly sliced
1 cup crumbled queso fresco

1. Combine the green onions, vinegar, ¼ cup cold water, the serranos, mayonnaise, sugar or honey, and oil in a blender and blend until emulsified; season with salt and pepper. Add the cilantro and pulse a few times just to incorporate.

2. Put the cabbage, carrot, and red onion in a bowl, add the green onion dressing, and stir until combined.

A savory coconut bath infuses lean pork tenderloin with rich flavor while it tenderizes the meat. With blazing heat akin to that of a Mexican habanero chile, the fruity Scotch bonnet chile is a quintessential Jamaican ingredient that drives home the Caribbean influence of this dish. The green onion–peanut relish adds an herbaceous crunch to the silky texture of the pork. Sometimes I pulse part of the relish in the food processor to make a chunky puree and leave the rest for sprinkling on top.

SERVES 4 TO 6

COCONUT-MARINATED PORK TENDERLOIN
||| **WITH** ||| *green onion–peanut relish*

1 (14-ounce) can unsweetened coconut milk
Grated zest of 2 limes
Juice of 2 limes
1 heaping tablespoon mild curry powder
2 teaspoons mild Spanish paprika
6 garlic cloves, finely chopped
3 tablespoons grated fresh ginger
1 Scotch bonnet chile, chopped, or 2 tablespoons Scotch bonnet hot sauce
¼ teaspoon coarsely ground black pepper
1 (2-pound) pork tenderloin, trimmed of excess fat
2 tablespoons canola oil
Kosher salt
4 green onions, green and pale green parts, halved lengthwise and finely chopped
2 tablespoons finely chopped fresh cilantro leaves
⅛ teaspoon ground allspice
½ cup coarsely chopped roasted peanuts
Hot sauce

1 Combine the coconut milk, lime zest, lime juice, curry powder, paprika, garlic, ginger, Scotch bonnet, and pepper in a bowl. Add the pork, turn to coat in the marinade, cover, and refrigerate for at least 2 hours and up to 8 hours.

2 Heat your grill to high for indirect grilling (see page 23). Remove the pork from the refrigerator 30 minutes before cooking and pat dry with paper towels.

3 Brush the pork with the oil and season with salt. Put the pork directly over the heat and cook until charred on all sides, about 8 minutes. Remove to the cooler part of the grill (indirect heat) and continue grilling until an instant-read thermometer inserted into the center of the pork registers 150°F, about 12 minutes longer.

4 Remove the pork from the grill, tent loosely with foil, and let rest for 10 minutes.

5 Combine the green onions, cilantro, allspice, and peanuts in a bowl and season with salt.

6 Slice the pork into ¼-inch-thick slices. Sprinkle with the green onion–peanut relish and serve with hot sauce.

*I am always doing my homework on vacation. Everything I eat and drink while traveling becomes possible inspiration for my next great dish. This pork dish is a result of a summertime trip to Sicily, which is home to the classic sour (*agro*) and sweet (*dolce*) sauce. The all-at-once sweet-sour-savory preparation is a perfect way to welcome the fruits of summer to your table. Pork and peaches are actually a classic combination.* **SERVES 4 TO 6**

1 (3- to 4-pound) pork loin with ⅛-inch
　　layer of fat
Honey and rosemary brine (see page 117)
Fresh rosemary or sage sprigs
5 tablespoons canola oil
Kosher salt and freshly ground black
　　pepper
3 slightly underripe peaches, halved
　　and pitted
1 cup red wine vinegar
¼ cup peach nectar or water
½ cup clover honey
Chopped fresh flat-leaf parsley leaves,
　　for garnish

GRILLED PORK LOIN
||| **WITH** ||| *agrodolce peaches*

1 Brine the pork loin in the honey-rosemary brine in the refrigerator for at least 4 hours and up to 12 hours.

2 Remove the pork from the brine, rinse under cold water, and pat dry with paper towels. Let sit at room temperature for 1 hour before cooking.

3 Soak 2 cups almond (or apple or cherry) wood chips and the rosemary sprigs in water for at least 30 minutes.

4 Heat your grill to high for indirect grilling (see page 23).

5 Add 1 cup of the drained wood chips to the coals in a charcoal grill or put them in a smoker box of a gas grill. Close the cover and let smoke build for 10 minutes.

6 Brush the entire loin with 3 tablespoons of the oil and season with pepper. Put the pork on the grill directly over the heat source and grill until charred on all sides, about 10 minutes. Move to the cooler side of the grill (indirect heat) and close the cover. Grill, turning as needed, until an instant-read thermometer inserted into the thickest part of the roast registers about 140°F. This will take anywhere from 30 to 45 minutes, depending on the thickness of the loin. Aim to keep the grill temperature at around 375°F. Add the remaining drained wood chips halfway through the cooking time and additional hot coals as needed.

7 Transfer the pork loin to a cutting board, tent loosely with foil, and let rest for 15 minutes.

8 Brush the cut side of the peaches with the remaining 2 tablespoons oil and put on the grill, cut side down. Grill until lightly golden brown, about 2 minutes. Remove the peaches from the grill and cut each half into quarters.

9 Bring the vinegar, peach nectar, and honey to a simmer in a large high-sided sauté pan over medium heat; season with salt and pepper. Add the peaches and cook until slightly soft and warmed through, about 3 minutes. Remove the peaches to a plate and continue simmering the liquid until slightly reduced, about 5 minutes.

10 Cut the pork into thick slices. Serve with the peaches and drizzle some of the reduced peach glaze over the meat. Garnish with parsley.

The island of Capri's signature dish—a delicious salad of fresh mozzarella, basil, and tomatoes—is transformed into a hearty relish when made with the grilled tomatoes and flavored with briny capers, acidic red wine vinegar, and slivers of red onion. It's a perfect accompaniment to grilled hot and sweet Italian sausages tucked into soft hoagie rolls. The fresh ingredients and simple yet sophisticated relish elevate this street food fare. **SERVES 4 TO 6**

ITALIAN SAUSAGE HOAGIES
||| W I T H ||| *caprese relish*

¾ pound sweet Italian sausage
¾ pound hot Italian sausage
1 pint yellow and red cherry tomatoes
Canola oil
Kosher salt and freshly ground black pepper
1 pound fresh mozzarella or 1 pint bocconcini, cut into ½-inch dice
1 small red onion, halved and thinly sliced
1 tablespoon brined capers, drained
¼ cup chopped fresh basil leaves
2 tablespoons chopped fresh flat-leaf parsley leaves
¼ cup red wine vinegar
¼ cup extra-virgin olive oil, plus more for the bread
4 to 6 soft hoagie rolls
2 garlic cloves, halved

1 Heat your grill to high for direct grilling (see page 23). If using wooden skewers, soak in water for at least 15 minutes.

2 Thread the tomatoes separately onto skewers. Brush the tomatoes and sausages with canola oil and season with salt and pepper. Grill the sausages until cooked through, golden brown, and slightly charred on both sides, about 5 minutes per side. Grill the tomatoes until slightly charred and soft, about 2 minutes per side. Remove the sausages to a platter and let rest for 5 minutes. Remove the tomatoes from the skewers, cut in half, and put in a bowl.

3 Add the mozzarella, red onion, capers, basil, parsley, vinegar, and olive oil to the tomatoes. Season with salt and pepper and toss to combine the caprese relish.

4 Slice open the rolls and put on the grill, cut side down. Grill until lightly golden brown, about 30 seconds. Remove the rolls and rub the surfaces with the garlic cloves. Drizzle with olive oil and season with salt and pepper.

5 Divide the sweet and hot sausages among the rolls, top with the caprese relish, and serve.

We can thank the South for this zesty dish. Chowchow relish is a chunky southern condiment made from tart green tomatoes (and/or cabbage in other instances), onions, mustard seeds, a balanced blend of sugar and vinegar, and sweet and hot peppers, which I like grilled for an extra layer of smoky flavor. Southerners serve their chowchow on anything from pinto beans to hot dogs, so grilled smoked sausages are a natural pairing. **SERVES 6 TO 8**

1 cup apple cider vinegar
3 tablespoons packed light brown sugar
2 teaspoons kosher salt
1 teaspoon yellow mustard seeds
1 teaspoon celery seeds
1 large red bell pepper
1 large yellow bell pepper
1 jalapeño
Canola oil
3 green tomatoes, halved, seeded, and diced
1 small red onion, halved and thinly sliced
2 tablespoons extra-virgin olive oil
Freshly ground black pepper
1½ pounds smoked pork sausage links (12 to 14 links)
12 soft hoagie buns or hot dog buns, lightly toasted
Whole grain mustard

SMOKED SAUSAGE ||| WITH |||
green tomato chowchow relish

1 Combine the vinegar, brown sugar, salt, mustard seeds, and celery seeds in a small saucepan. Bring to a boil and cook until the brown sugar is dissolved, about 2 minutes. Remove from the heat and let cool completely.

2 Heat your grill to high for direct grilling (see page 23).

3 Brush the bell peppers and jalapeño with canola oil and grill, turning, until charred all over, about 10 minutes. Remove to a bowl, cover, and let sit for 10 minutes. Peel, seed, and roughly chop the bell peppers and jalapeño.

4 Combine the bell peppers, jalapeño, tomatoes, and red onion in a medium bowl. Add the cooled vinegar mixture, the olive oil, and black pepper and mix until combined. Cover and refrigerate the chowchow for at least 1 hour and up to 24 hours before serving.

5 Heat your grill to high for direct grilling (see page 23).

6 Grill the sausages until golden brown and charred on all sides and just cooked through, about 10 minutes.

7 Put a sausage on each bun and top with mustard and some of the chowchow.

The po'boy is how New Orleanians do lunch. This version of Louisiana's favorite sandwich is a winner—soft rolls grilled to golden and stuffed with spicy, super-smoky andouille sausage and sweet and snappy pickles. The spicy aioli is made with tangy Creole mustard, a nod to the traditional accompaniment, adding just another layer of authentic flavor for this mouthwatering and vibrant sandwich.

SERVES 4 TO 6

GRILLED ANDOUILLE SAUSAGE PO'BOYS ||| WITH ||| *spicy aioli* ||| AND ||| *quick pickles*

1 cup mayonnaise

1 heaping tablespoon Creole mustard

1 garlic clove, smashed to a paste

1 teaspoon mild Spanish paprika

¼ teaspoon cayenne

Kosher salt and freshly ground black pepper

1 pound uncooked andouille links, sliced lengthwise

4 demi baguettes or soft hoagie rolls, split

Thinly sliced tomatoes

Quick Bread-and-Butter Pickles (recipe follows)

1 To make the aioli, whisk together the mayonnaise, mustard, garlic, paprika, and cayenne in a bowl; season with salt and pepper. Cover and refrigerate for at least 30 minutes and up to 24 hours.

2 Soak 1 cup mesquite wood chips in water for at least 30 minutes.

3 Heat your grill to high for direct grilling (see page 23).

4 Add the drained wood chips to the coals in a charcoal grill or put them in a smoker box of a gas grill. Close the cover and let smoke build for 10 minutes,

5 Add the sausages, close the cover, and cook, turning several times, until slightly charred on both sides and cooked through, 12 to 15 minutes. Remove to a platter and let rest for a few minutes.

6 Spread 1 tablespoon of the aioli on the top and bottom of each roll and season with salt and pepper. Put the rolls on the grill, aioli side down. Grill until lightly golden brown, about 20 seconds.

7 Put a few slices of tomato on the bottom of each roll, top with the sausage and some of the pickles, and finally add the roll top. Serve immediately.

recipe continues >>

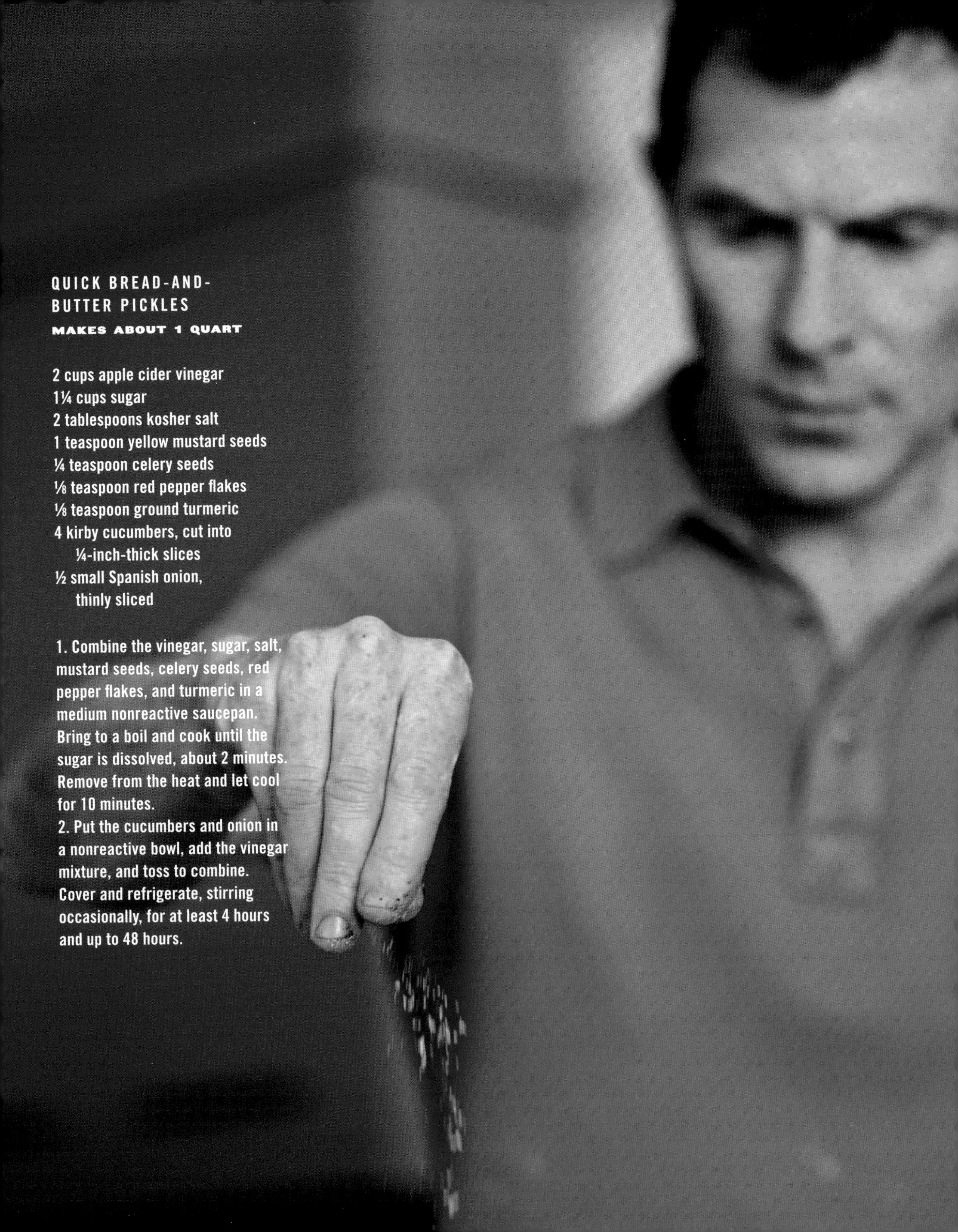

QUICK BREAD-AND-BUTTER PICKLES

MAKES ABOUT 1 QUART

2 cups apple cider vinegar
1¼ cups sugar
2 tablespoons kosher salt
1 teaspoon yellow mustard seeds
¼ teaspoon celery seeds
⅛ teaspoon red pepper flakes
⅛ teaspoon ground turmeric
4 kirby cucumbers, cut into
    ¼-inch-thick slices
½ small Spanish onion,
    thinly sliced

1. Combine the vinegar, sugar, salt, mustard seeds, celery seeds, red pepper flakes, and turmeric in a medium nonreactive saucepan. Bring to a boil and cook until the sugar is dissolved, about 2 minutes. Remove from the heat and let cool for 10 minutes.

2. Put the cucumbers and onion in a nonreactive bowl, add the vinegar mixture, and toss to combine. Cover and refrigerate, stirring occasionally, for at least 4 hours and up to 48 hours.

Fondue—it's a throwback and I'm loving it. It's a fun dish made for sharing and definitely for indulging. Serve it alongside the Beer-Simmered Bratwurst Sandwiches and use the bratwurst-infused beer cooking liquid in the fondue's base for an extra layer of smoky, savory flavor. **SERVES 4 TO 6**

SMOKED CHEESE ||| AND ||| BEER FONDUE

10 ounces grated sharp white cheddar cheese (2½ cups)

6 ounces grated Gruyère cheese (about 1½ cups)

2 ounces smoked Swiss or Gruyère cheese, shredded (about ½ cup)

Scant 1 tablespoon cornstarch

2 cups strained beer brat cooking liquid (see page 167)

2 tablespoons spicy brown mustard

Few dashes of hot sauce

Kosher salt and freshly ground black pepper

Rye bread cubes

Baby carrots

Radishes

Cherry tomatoes

Cornichons

1 Combine the cheddar, Gruyère, and Swiss in a large bowl and toss with the cornstarch.

2 Bring the cooking liquid to a simmer in a medium saucepan, add the cheeses a few handfuls at a time, and stir in a figure eight with a wooden spoon until smooth. Whisk in the mustard and hot sauce and season with salt and pepper if needed.

3 Serve warm with the rye bread, carrots, radishes, tomatoes, and cornichons for dipping.

This is just right on a cool autumn night. And as for you Oktoberfest fans, look no further for your perfect dish. This is a fairly traditional preparation for "brats" and onions with one delicious twist: Instead of serving it with a long-cooked sauerkraut, I opt for a fresh and crunchy coleslaw that hits the same sweet-and-sour notes.

SERVES 8

BEER-SIMMERED BRATWURST SANDWICHES ⫴ WITH ⫴ *onions* ⫴ AND ⫴ *sweet-and-sour slaw*

3 large Spanish onions, thinly sliced
3 pounds precooked bratwurst, pricked with a fork
4 (12-ounce) bottles German light ale
1 teaspoon coriander seeds
1 teaspoon caraway seeds
1 teaspoon yellow mustard seeds
1 (2-inch) piece fresh ginger, peeled and chopped
3 garlic cloves, smashed
2 tablespoons canola oil
12 to 16 soft hoagie buns or hot dog buns, lightly toasted
Sweet and hot German mustard
Spicy brown mustard
Sweet and Sour Slaw (recipe follows)
Fresh flat-leaf parsley leaves, for garnish

1 Heat your grill to high for direct grilling (see page 23).

2 Arrange the onion slices on the bottom of a medium stockpot. Put the bratwurst on top and add the beer, 2 cups water, the coriander seeds, caraway seeds, mustard seeds, ginger, and garlic. Put the pot on the grates of the grill and bring to a simmer. Turn off the heat, close the cover, and let sit for 30 minutes.

3 Transfer the bratwurst to a platter and brush them with the oil. Put the onions in a bowl. Strain the liquid into a bowl to use for fondue (see page 165); discard the solids.

4 Grill the bratwursts until the casings are crisp and browned, 4 to 6 minutes per side.

5 Serve the brats on buns topped with the mustards, onions, Sweet-and-Sour Slaw, and parsley.

SWEET-AND-SOUR SLAW
MAKES ENOUGH TO TOP 16 SANDWICHES

1 cup apple cider vinegar
½ cup superfine sugar
2 tablespoons grated Spanish onion
2 teaspoons dry mustard
1 teaspoon celery seeds
1 teaspoon celery salt
Kosher salt and freshly ground black pepper
1 cup canola oil
1 medium head cabbage, finely shredded
2 large carrots, shredded

Whisk together the vinegar and sugar in a large bowl until the sugar dissolves. Add the onion, dry mustard, celery seeds, and celery salt and season with kosher salt and pepper. Slowly whisk in the oil until emulsified. Add the cabbage and carrot and toss to combine. Let sit at room temperature for at least 15 minutes before serving.

To many Americans, barbecue sauce is red, sweet, and smoky—end of story. But there's a whole barbecue culture out there that knows that is just the tip of the barbecue iceberg. Sauces vary by region, and the one for this succulent sandwich is from the eastern reaches of North Carolina. It's a vinegar-based sauce, nicely acidic and seasoned with red flecks of ancho and cayenne chile powders. Those North Carolinians are up to something: I just love how the tangy sauce complements the smoky pulled pork. A pile of crunchy coleslaw finishes the sandwich with a great contrasting texture and fresh flavor. Because of the long cooking time, a smoker is ideal for this recipe, or a charcoal (not gas) grill. **SERVES 6 TO 8**

SMOKED PULLED PORK
||| **WITH** ||| *north carolina*
barbecue sauce ||| **AND** ||| *tangy slaw*

PORK

1 (4-pound) pork butt
6 tablespoons ancho chile powder
3 tablespoons mild Spanish paprika
2 tablespoons ground oregano
2 tablespoons ground coriander
2 tablespoons dry mustard
1 tablespoon ground cumin
1 teaspoon chile de árbol powder or
    cayenne
Kosher salt and freshly ground black
    pepper

BARBECUE SAUCE

3 cups apple cider vinegar
½ cup ketchup
2 tablespoons ancho chile powder
2 tablespoons packed light brown sugar
1½ teaspoons kosher salt
1 teaspoon freshly ground black pepper
¼ teaspoon cayenne or chile de árbol
    powder

12 soft hamburger buns
Tangy Slaw (recipe follows)
Sour pickle slices, optional

1 Marinate the pork: Put the pork, fat side up, on a large baking sheet. Combine all the spices, herbs, 2 tablespoons salt, and 1 tablespoon pepper and rub all over the pork, pressing them into the pork. Cover with plastic wrap and refrigerate for at least 4 hours and up to 24 hours.

2 Make the barbecue sauce: Combine the vinegar, ketchup, ancho powder, brown sugar, salt, pepper, and cayenne in a medium saucepan and bring to a boil over high heat. Cook for 1 minute. Remove from the heat and let cool to room temperature. Divide the sauce between 2 bowls, reserving half for mopping and half for serving. (The sauce can be made 1 week in advance and kept, covered, in the refrigerator. Bring to room temperature before using.)

3 Remove the pork from the refrigerator 1 hour before cooking.

4 Soak 2 cups of hickory chips in water for at least 30 minutes.

5 Heat your smoker according to the manufacturer's instructions. If using a charcoal grill, set up a drip pan with water on the bottom grates and heat the grill to low for indirect grilling (see page 23). Put half of the drained wood chips over the hot coals, add the cooking grate, and close the cover. Open the vents halfway and maintain a temperature between 225°F and 250°F. Let smoke build for 10 minutes.

6 Season the pork all over with salt and pepper and add to the smoker or grill over the pan filled with water, close the cover, and smoke for 1 hour. Baste the pork with the barbecue sauce and continue to

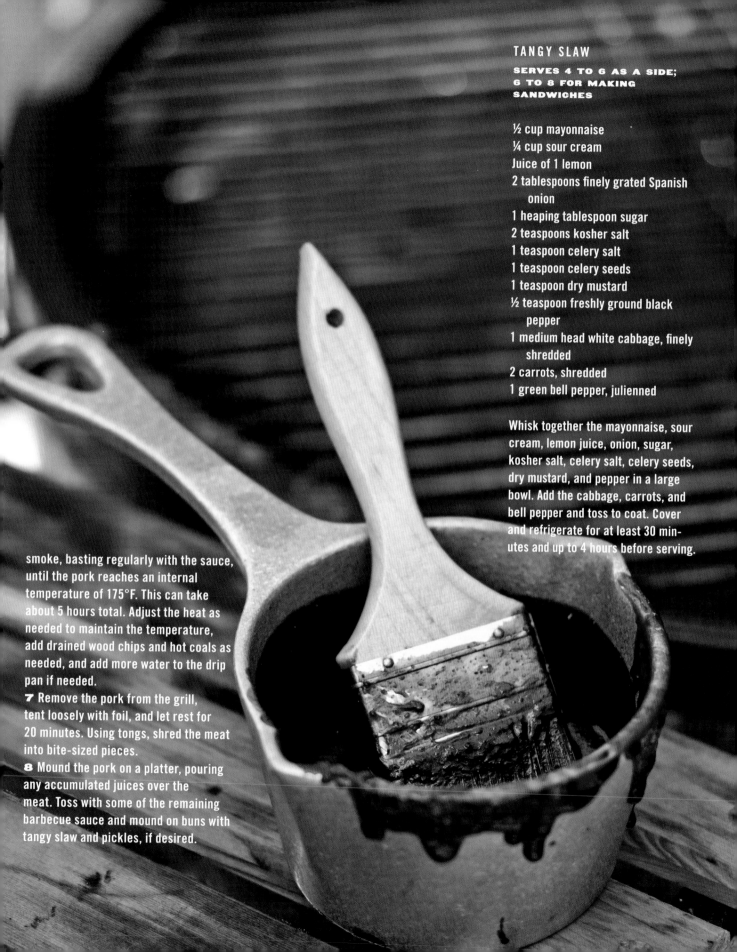

TANGY SLAW

SERVES 4 TO 6 AS A SIDE;
6 TO 8 FOR MAKING
SANDWICHES

½ cup mayonnaise
¼ cup sour cream
Juice of 1 lemon
2 tablespoons finely grated Spanish
   onion
1 heaping tablespoon sugar
2 teaspoons kosher salt
1 teaspoon celery salt
1 teaspoon celery seeds
1 teaspoon dry mustard
½ teaspoon freshly ground black
   pepper
1 medium head white cabbage, finely
   shredded
2 carrots, shredded
1 green bell pepper, julienned

Whisk together the mayonnaise, sour
cream, lemon juice, onion, sugar,
kosher salt, celery salt, celery seeds,
dry mustard, and pepper in a large
bowl. Add the cabbage, carrots, and
bell pepper and toss to coat. Cover
and refrigerate for at least 30 minutes and up to 4 hours before serving.

smoke, basting regularly with the sauce,
until the pork reaches an internal
temperature of 175°F. This can take
about 5 hours total. Adjust the heat as
needed to maintain the temperature,
add drained wood chips and hot coals as
needed, and add more water to the drip
pan if needed.

7 Remove the pork from the grill,
tent loosely with foil, and let rest for
20 minutes. Using tongs, shred the meat
into bite-sized pieces.

8 Mound the pork on a platter, pouring
any accumulated juices over the
meat. Toss with some of the remaining
barbecue sauce and mound on buns with
tangy slaw and pickles, if desired.

BEEF AND

LAMB

When you think barbecue, you gotta think brisket. With a flavorful rub that needs at least 4 hours and up to 24 to permeate the meat with its smoky, spicy flavor—and then 9 hours in the smoker—this is the epitome of low and slow cooking. You need a smoker or charcoal (not gas) grill to pull off this recipe in true barbecue style. Brisket is a tough cut—there's no quick medium-rare on this thing—but as the fat slowly melts, it bastes the brisket until it's super tender and moist. Trust me: It's worth every minute of waiting. **SERVES 8**

SMOKED SPICE-RUBBED BRISKET, TEXAS STYLE, ON TEXAS TOAST

TEXAS MOP
1 tablespoon canola oil
½ teaspoon fennel seeds
½ teaspoon coriander seeds
½ teaspoon cumin seeds
½ teaspoon red pepper flakes
2 garlic cloves, chopped
1 cup apple cider vinegar
3 tablespoons packed light brown sugar
1 tablespoon Worcestershire sauce
1 teaspoon kosher salt
¼ teaspoon freshly ground black pepper
2 cups ketchup
Scant ¼ cup fresh cilantro leaves

BRISKET
3 tablespoons ancho chile powder
1 tablespoon garlic powder
1 tablespoon dried oregano
1 tablespoon celery seeds
1 tablespoon mild Spanish paprika
1 tablespoon coriander seeds, ground
1 tablespoon yellow mustard seeds, ground
1 tablespoon allspice berries, ground
1 tablespoon freshly ground black pepper
2 tablespoons kosher salt
1 (8- to 10-pound) brisket with ¼-inch layer of fat on top
2 cups apple juice, in a spray bottle, or more if needed

Grilled Texas Toast (recipe follows)

1 Make the mop: Heat the oil in a medium saucepan over medium heat until it begins to shimmer. Add the fennel seeds, coriander seeds, cumin seeds, and red pepper flakes and cook, stirring constantly, for 1 minute. Add the garlic and cook for 30 seconds. Add the vinegar, brown sugar, Worcestershire, salt, pepper, ketchup, and 1 cup water and simmer, stirring occasionally, until slightly thickened, about 20 minutes.

2 Transfer the mixture to a blender, add the cilantro, and blend until smooth. Pour into a bowl and serve warm. (The mop can be made 2 days in advance and stored, covered, in the refrigerator. Reheat gently before using.)

3 Marinate the brisket: Mix together all the spices, herbs, and salt in a bowl. Liberally rub the entire brisket with the

mixture, wrap tightly in plastic wrap, and refrigerate for at least 4 hours and up to 24 hours.

4 Remove the brisket from the refrigerator 1 hour before cooking.

5 Soak 3 cups oak or pecan wood chips in water for at least 30 minutes.

6 Heat your smoker according to the manufacturer's instructions. If using a charcoal grill, set up a drip pan with water on the bottom grates and heat the grill to low for indirect grilling (see page 23). Put half of the drained wood chips over the hot coals, add the cooking grate, and close the cover. Open the vents halfway and maintain a temperature between 225°F and 250°F. Let smoke build for 10 minutes.

7 Put the brisket, fat side up, in the smoker or grill over the pan filled with water. Close the cover and smoke, spraying every 30 minutes with apple juice, until the meat starts to get tender and reaches an internal temperature of 165°F to 170°F, about 6 hours. Adjust the heat as needed to maintain the temperature, add drained wood chips and hot coals as needed, and add more water to the drip pan if needed.

8 Wrap the entire brisket in foil and return it to the smoker until an instant-read thermometer easily slides into the meat and the internal temperature registers 185°F, 2 to 3 hours. (This little trick—wrapping the brisket in foil—is a big help in getting the meat tender, especially for beginners.) Adjust the heat as needed to maintain the temperature, add drained wood chips and hot coals as needed, and add more water to the drip pan if needed.

9 Remove the brisket packet from the smoker and let rest for 20 minutes.

10 Remove the foil from the brisket over a large pan and reserve the liquid. If desired, cut off the brisket points and reserve for baked beans (see page 105). Thinly slice the brisket across the grain. Serve on Texas toast, if desired, topped with some of the mop sauce and reserved cooking juices.

GRILLED TEXAS TOAST
SERVES 8

2 teaspoons canola oil
4 garlic cloves, smashed to a paste
½ pound (2 sticks) unsalted butter, softened
Kosher salt and freshly ground black pepper
2 loaves good-quality Pullman white bread, cut into 1-inch-thick slices
2 tablespoons finely chopped fresh flat-leaf parsley leaves, for garnish

1. Heat your grill to high for direct grilling (see page 23).
2. Heat the oil in a small sauté pan, add the garlic, and cook for 1 minute. Let cool slightly. Stir in the butter and season with salt and pepper.
3. Grill the bread until lightly golden brown on both sides. Remove from the grill and spread one side of each slice with some of the garlic butter. Place on a platter and sprinkle with the parsley.

What could be more all-American than prime rib? Tender, juicy, and full of flavor, prime rib is the way to celebrate a special occasion in this country. This recipe produces a fantastic crust, which many traditional preparations lack. A good dose of spice rub as well as a two-part cooking process that starts over direct heat give a gorgeous exterior that creates such an awesome contrast to the luscious meat inside. Cook this recipe on a dedicated smoker or a charcoal (not gas) grill. The red wine steak sauce will become a favorite for any steak—make extra so that you always have some in the fridge. **SERVES 6 TO 8**

SMOKED PRIME RIB
||| WITH ||| *red wine steak sauce*

PRIME RIB
1 (6- to 8-pound) 4-rib prime rib roast, untrimmed
1 cup Bobby Flay's Spice Rub for Pork and Beef (see Sources) or your favorite rub for beef
Kosher salt

RED WINE STEAK SAUCE
2 tablespoons canola oil
2 shallots, chopped
2 garlic cloves, chopped
2 plum tomatoes, chopped
1 cup dry red wine

2 tablespoons molasses
2 tablespoons packed light brown sugar
¼ cup raisins
1 cup ketchup
2 heaping tablespoons Dijon mustard
3 heaping tablespoons prepared horseradish
1 tablespoon Worcestershire sauce
Pinch of cayenne
Kosher salt and freshly ground black pepper
2 tablespoons red wine vinegar

recipe continues >>

1 Marinate the prime rib: Rub the prime rib with the spice rub, put on a baking rack set over a baking sheet, and refrigerate, uncovered, for at least 4 hours and up to 8 hours.

2 Make the steak sauce: Heat the oil in a medium saucepan over medium heat. Add the shallots and cook until soft, about 2 minutes. Add the garlic and cook for 30 seconds. Add the tomatoes, increase the heat to high, and cook until softened and the liquid has evaporated, about 5 minutes.

3 Add the wine and cook until reduced by half. Add the molasses, brown sugar, raisins, and ½ cup water and cook for 5 minutes. Add the ketchup, mustard, horseradish, Worcestershire, and the cayenne; season with salt and pepper and simmer for 5 minutes. Transfer to a blender and blend until smooth. Add the vinegar and transfer to a bowl. Let cool to room temperature.

4 Soak 2 cups hickory wood chips in water for at least 30 minutes.

5 Remove the prime rib from the refrigerator 1 hour before cooking and let sit at room temperature.

6 Heat your smoker according to the manufacturer's instructions. If using a charcoal grill, set up a drip pan with water on the bottom grates and heat the grill to low for indirect grilling (see page 23). Put half of the drained wood chips over the hot coals, add the cooking grate, and close the cover. Open the vents halfway and maintain a temperature between 225°F and 250°F. Let smoke build for 10 minutes.

7 Season the prime rib well with salt and put it, fat side up, on the smoker or grill over the pan filled with water. Close the cover and smoke for 2½ hours. Adjust the heat as needed to maintain the temperature, add drained wood chips and hot coals as needed, and add more water to the drip pan if needed.

8 After 2½ hours, baste with some of the steak sauce and continue to cook, basting every 15 minutes, until an instant-read thermometer inserted into the center of the roast registers 130°F, 1 to 1½ hours more.

9 Remove the prime rib from the grill and brush with more of the sauce. Tent loosely with foil and let rest for 20 minutes before slicing.

This is so aromatic; you can smell the garlic in the marinade the instant the steak hits the grill. I think of Cuban food as reinforcement cooking because you see many of the same ingredients (think garlic, oregano, cumin) played out in a multitude of dishes. It's definitely positive reinforcement—it's all delicious. Tomato escabeche is a fresh salsa or relish served with all sorts of traditional Cuban dishes. A puree of ripe mangoes thickens and flavors the savory steak sauce. **SERVES 4**

CUBAN SKIRT STEAK
WITH *tomato escabeche* AND
mango steak sauce

SKIRT STEAK
8 garlic cloves, chopped
¼ cup chopped fresh oregano
2 fresh bay leaves (not dried)
1 teaspoon cumin seeds, toasted
Grated zest of 2 limes
Juice of 2 limes
¼ cup canola oil
1½ pounds skirt steak, cut into
    2 or 3 pieces crosswise
Kosher salt and freshly ground black
    pepper

TOMATO ESCABECHE
3 ripe beefsteak tomatoes, halved, pulp
    and seeds removed, and flesh cut into
    thin strips
1 small red onion, halved and thinly sliced
1 jalapeño, julienned
3 tablespoons red wine vinegar
2 tablespoons fresh lime juice
1 teaspoon sugar
¼ cup chopped fresh cilantro leaves
Kosher salt and freshly ground black
    pepper

Mango Steak Sauce (recipe follows)
Chopped fresh cilantro leaves, for
    garnish

recipe continues >>

1 Marinate the steak: Combine the garlic, oregano, bay leaves, cumin seeds, lime zest, lime juice, and oil in a blender and blend until smooth. Put the steak in a large baking dish, add the marinade, cover, and refrigerate for at least 4 hours and up to 24 hours.

2 Heat your grill to high for direct grilling (see page 23). Thirty minutes before cooking, remove the steak from the refrigerator and from the marinade and transfer to a plate.

3 Make the tomato escabeche: Combine the tomatoes, red onion, jalapeño, vinegar, lime juice, sugar, and cilantro in a bowl. Season with salt and pepper. Cover and let sit at room temperature for at least 30 minutes.

4 Season the steaks with salt and pepper on both sides. Grill on both sides until golden brown, slightly charred, and cooked to medium-rare, about 5 minutes per side. Remove the steaks to a cutting board, tent loosely with foil, and let rest for 10 minutes.

5 Cut the steak against the grain and serve topped with the tomato escabeche. Garnish with chopped cilantro. Serve the mango steak sauce on the side.

MANGO STEAK SAUCE
MAKES ABOUT 2 CUPS

2 tablespoons canola oil
1 small red onion, chopped
2 garlic cloves, chopped
2 very ripe mangoes, peeled, pitted, and chopped
½ cup mango nectar
2 tablespoons ancho chile powder
¼ cup prepared horseradish
2 tablespoons clover honey
2 tablespoons Dijon mustard
2 tablespoons pure grade B maple syrup
2 teaspoons Worcestershire sauce
Kosher salt and freshly ground black pepper

1. Heat the oil in a medium high-sided skillet over medium-high heat. Add the onion and cook until soft, about 5 minutes. Add the garlic and cook for 30 seconds. Add the mangoes, mango nectar, and ancho powder and cook, stirring occasionally, until the mangoes are very soft and the mixture has thickened, about 15 minutes.

2. Transfer the mixture to a food processor or blender. Add the horseradish, honey, mustard, maple syrup, and Worcestershire; season with salt and pepper and blend until smooth. Scrape the sauce into a bowl and let cool to room temperature.

Steak and potatoes, Spanish style. These wrinkled potatoes, a specialty of Spain's Canary Islands, are at once firm but tender and have a great, true potato flavor. Traditionally the potatoes are boiled in heavily salted water until they emerge wrinkled and covered in a film of salt; they are delicious that way, but I like the touch of smoke they pick up from the wood chips' smoke and the flame of the grill. Chile-spiked mojo rojo, *or red sauce, is the classic accompaniment and works just as well with a nice bit of juicy grilled strip steak.* **SERVES 4 TO 6**

2 (1-pound) New York strip steaks, each
    1½ inches thick
2½ pounds small new potatoes, red,
    white, or a mixture
Kosher salt and freshly ground black
    pepper
6 tablespoons canola oil
Garlic Aioli (recipe follows)
Mojo Rojo (recipe follows)
Chopped fresh flat-leaf parsley leaves,
    for garnish

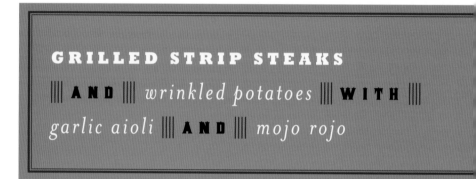

GRILLED STRIP STEAKS
||| **AND** ||| *wrinkled potatoes* ||| **WITH** |||
garlic aioli ||| **AND** ||| *mojo rojo*

1 Soak 1 cup hickory wood chips in water for at least 30 minutes.

2 Remove the steaks from the refrigerator while the potatoes cook.

3 Put the potatoes in a large saucepan, add cold water to cover by 2 inches, and stir in 2 tablespoons salt. Bring to a boil, cover, and cook until tender, about 15 minutes. Drain well.

4 Heat your grill to high for indirect grilling (see page 23).

5 Add the drained wood chips to the coals in a charcoal grill or put them in a smoker box of a gas grill. Close the cover and let smoke build for 10 minutes.

6 Brush the steaks on both sides with 2 tablespoons of the oil and season with salt and pepper. Put the steaks directly over the coals and grill until golden brown and a crust has formed, about 5 minutes. Turn over the steaks and cook until the bottoms are golden brown, about 4 minutes. Move to the cooler part of the grill (indirect heat) and continue grilling until cooked to medium-rare, about 5 minutes. Transfer the steaks to a cutting board, tent loosely with foil, and let rest for 10 minutes.

7 While the steak is resting, toss the potatoes in the remaining 4 tablespoons oil and season with pepper. Grill over direct heat, turning constantly, until the skins get lightly golden brown and crisp, about 5 minutes.

8 Slice the steak into thick slices and arrange with the potatoes on a platter. Serve the aioli and mojo on the side. Garnish with parsley.

recipe continues >>

GARLIC AIOLI
MAKES ABOUT 1 CUP

1 cup mayonnaise
1 teaspoon fresh lemon juice
6 garlic cloves, smashed to a paste
Kosher salt and freshly ground black
    pepper

Stir together the mayonnaise, lemon
juice, and garlic and season with salt and
pepper. Cover and refrigerate for at least
1 hour before serving to allow the flavors
to meld.

MOJO ROJO
MAKES ABOUT ⅔ CUP

4 garlic cloves
1 tablespoon mild Spanish paprika
1 teaspoon hot Spanish paprika or
    ½ teaspoon cayenne or chile de árbol
    powder
¼ teaspoon cumin seeds
1 teaspoon kosher salt
¼ teaspoon freshly ground black pepper
2 tablespoons red wine vinegar
½ cup extra-virgin olive oil

Combine the garlic, both paprikas, the
cumin seeds, salt, and pepper in a mortar
and smash with a pestle until smooth or
pulse to a paste in a small food processor. Add the vinegar and oil and mix until
blended.

Argentineans love fresh and garlicky chimichurri with just about anything, but in my mind it is best paired with a flavorful grilled skirt steak. This dish utilizes a duo of the classic sauces: traditional green chimichurri as a marinade for the steak to infuse it with flavor, and red chimichurri, poured atop the grilled steak before serving. The red chimichurri gets its hue from fresh tomatoes, smoked paprika, and smoky, fruity chipotle puree, which add depth and heat to this herbaceous sauce. **SERVES 4**

GRILLED SKIRT STEAK
WITH green AND smoky red chimichurri

recipe continues >>

SKIRT STEAK
16 garlic cloves
2 cups fresh flat-leaf parsley leaves
1 cup fresh oregano leaves
1 cup fresh mint leaves
2 teaspoons red pepper flakes
½ cup red wine vinegar
1 cup canola oil
Kosher salt and freshly ground black pepper
1½ pounds skirt steak, cut crosswise into 3 pieces

RED CHIMICHURRI
1 small red onion, finely diced
3 garlic cloves, finely chopped
¼ cup aged sherry vinegar or red wine vinegar
2 plum tomatoes, halved, seeded, and chopped
1 tablespoon pureed canned chipotle in adobo
1 tablespoon smoked mild paprika
1 cup finely chopped fresh flat-leaf parsley leaves
2 tablespoons finely chopped fresh oregano
½ cup extra-virgin olive oil
Kosher salt and freshly ground black pepper

1 Marinate the skirt steak in the green chimichurri: Combine the garlic, parsley, oregano, mint, red pepper flakes, vinegar, and canola oil in a food processor and process until smooth. Put the steak in a large baking dish, add half of the green chimichurri sauce, and turn to coat. Cover and refrigerate for at least 4 hours and up to 24 hours. Refrigerate the remaining sauce separately.

2 Heat your grill or parilla to high for direct grilling (see page 23). Thirty minutes before cooking, remove the steak from the refrigerator and transfer to a plate. Discard the marinade.

3 Make the red chimichurri: Using a mortar with a pestle, combine the onion, garlic, vinegar, tomatoes, chipotle, paprika, parsley, oregano, and olive oil. Season with salt and pepper.

4 Season the steaks with salt and pepper on both sides. Grill until charred on both sides and cooked to medium-rare, about 5 minutes per side. Remove the steaks to a cutting board, tent loosely with foil, and let rest for 5 minutes.

5 Cut the meat across the grain into thin slices and top with red chimichurri and the reserved green chimichurri.

Rib eyes are the kind of steak I often order when I'm out. They have the most flavor, which comes from all that gorgeous marbling. This dish may sound like a crazy combination, but I have to tell you, it works. I just love the way the tangy goat cheese, bright mustard, and fresh peppery watercress come together to complement the rich beefiness of these thick steaks. As a matter of fact, I think it works so well that I serve a burger with these same toppings at Bobby's Burger Palace; the Napa burger is one of my favorites. If you can't find Meyer lemons, just use the zest and juice of half of a regular lemon and half of an orange instead. **SERVES 4**

RIB EYE ||| WITH ||| *goat cheese*
||| AND ||| *meyer lemon—honey mustard*

1 (2-pound) rib eye, 1½ inches thick,
    excess fat trimmed
½ cup clover honey
1 tablespoon Dijon mustard
1 tablespoon whole grain mustard
Grated zest and juice of 1 Meyer lemon
4 ounces fresh goat cheese, slightly
    softened
Kosher salt and freshly ground black
    pepper
Canola oil
Fresh flat-leaf parsley leaves, for garnish

1 Remove the steak from the refrigerator 30 minutes before cooking.

2 Whisk together the honey, both mustards, the lemon zest, and lemon juice in a small bowl and let the mixture sit at room temperature for at least 30 minutes to allow the flavors to meld.

3 Put the goat cheese in a bowl and season with salt and pepper. Refrigerate until needed.

4 Heat your grill to high for indirect grilling (see page 23).

5 Brush the steak with canola oil and season liberally with salt and pepper. Grill, directly over the coals, until golden brown and slightly charred, about 5 minutes. Turn over the steak and position it away from the coals (indirect heat). Close the cover and grill, turning once, until an instant-read thermometer inserted into the center registers 135°F, about 10 minutes. Remove the steak from the grill to a cutting board, tent loosely with foil, and let rest for 5 minutes.

6 Top the steak with the goat cheese, drizzle with the honey mustard, and garnish with parsley leaves.

Thick molasses and dark rum combine in this complex, sweet-and-spicy glaze with a luxurious consistency. Smoky, fruity ancho chiles add spice and body to the rich glaze. For a delightful contrast, I like to serve this with a crisp and bright salad of peppery radish and crunchy jicama, seasoned with sunny grapefruit juice and fresh ginger. **SERVES 4**

2 dried ancho chiles
2 tablespoons canola oil, plus more for brushing
1 large shallot, finely diced
3 garlic cloves, finely chopped
1 cup Myers's dark rum
2 cups low-sodium chicken broth
2 tablespoons molasses
2 tablespoons packed dark brown sugar
½ teaspoon coarsely ground black pepper
Pinch of cayenne
Kosher salt
1 tablespoon apple cider vinegar
2 (16- to 18-ounce) bone-in rib eyes, each 1½ inches thick
Jicama-Radish Salad with Grapefruit-Ginger Vinaigrette (page 87)

SPICY MOLASSES-RUM-GLAZED RIB EYES ||| WITH |||
jicama-radish salad

1 Put the ancho chiles in a small bowl, cover with 1 cup boiling water, and let sit until softened, about 30 minutes. Drain, reserving the soaking liquid. Remove the stems and seeds from the chiles, transfer the chiles to a blender or food processor with ½ cup of the soaking liquid, and process until smooth.

2 Heat the oil in a medium saucepan over medium-high heat. Add the shallot and garlic and cook until soft, about 2 minutes. Pour in the rum and boil until almost completely reduced, about 5 minutes. Add the chicken broth, ancho puree, molasses, and brown sugar and cook until reduced by half and thickened, about 10 minutes. Season the glaze with the black pepper, cayenne, salt, and vinegar. Let cool to room temperature.

3 Remove the steaks from the refrigerator 30 minutes before cooking.

4 Heat your grill to high for direct grilling (see page 23).

5 Brush the steaks with oil and season with salt. Put the steaks on the grill and cook until golden brown and a crust has formed, about 5 minutes. Flip over the steaks, brush with some of the rum glaze, and grill until the bottoms are golden brown, about 4 minutes. Flip again and cook until medium-rare, about 2 minutes more.

6 Transfer the steaks, glaze side up, to a cutting board and brush with more of the glaze. Tent loosely with foil and let rest for 5 minutes before slicing. Serve with the jicama-radish salad.

Tuscan porterhouse, or bistecca alla fiorentia, *is a showstopper of a steak. Grilled on the bone and traditionally served rare, this cut gives you fantastic beefy flavor on the strip side as well as a tender fillet. A rich blend of Tuscan ingredients such as fragrant rosemary and sweetly acidic balsamic vinegar blend into a mouthwatering steak sauce. Treviso is a mild variety of the Italian lettuce radicchio. Its long, deep red leaves have a crinkly texture and a slightly bitter, nutty flavor that mellows with the grill's heat.* **SERVES 4 TO 6**

¼ cup canola oil, plus more for drizzling
4 garlic cloves, finely chopped
2 tablespoons finely chopped fresh
    rosemary
2 (16-ounce) porterhouse steaks, each
    1½ inches thick
Kosher salt and freshly ground black
    pepper
Balsamic-Rosemary Steak Sauce (recipe
    follows)
2 heads Treviso
Balsamic vinegar
Extra-virgin olive oil
4 ounces crumbled Gorgonzola
Fresh flat-leaf parsley leaves, for garnish
Fresh rosemary, for garnish

TUSCAN PORTERHOUSE
||| **WITH** ||| *balsamic-rosemary steak sauce* ||| **AND** ||| *grilled treviso*

1 Marinate the steaks: Whisk together the canola oil, garlic, and chopped rosemary in a large baking dish. Add the steaks and turn to coat in the marinade. Cover and refrigerate for at least 1 hour and up to 12 hours.

2 Soak 1 cup almond wood chips in water for at least 30 minutes.

3 Remove the steaks from the refrigerator 30 minutes before cooking.

4 Heat your grill to high for direct grilling (see page 23). Add the drained wood chips to the coals in a charcoal grill or put them in a smoker box of a gas grill. Close the cover and let smoke build for 10 minutes.

5 Remove the steaks from the marinade and pat dry. Season both sides liberally with salt and pepper. Grill until charred on both sides and cooked to medium, 5 to 6 minutes per side. Remove the steaks from the grill and drizzle with a little of the steak sauce. Tent loosely with foil and let sit for 5 minutes before slicing.

6 While the steaks are resting, drizzle the Treviso with canola oil and season with salt and pepper. Grill until slightly charred and wilted, about 1 minute. Flip over and grill for 1 minute just to heat through.

7 Put the Treviso on a platter, drizzle with a little balsamic and some olive oil, and add the Gorgonzola. Top with slices of the steak and drizzle with more steak sauce. Garnish with parsley and rosemary.

BALSAMIC-ROSEMARY STEAK SAUCE

MAKES ABOUT 1 CUP

2 cups balsamic vinegar
2 garlic cloves, smashed
3 fresh rosemary sprigs
1 large grilled or jarred roasted red bell
    pepper, peeled, seeded, and diced
2 tablespoons prepared horseradish
2 tablespoons clover honey
1 tablespoon molasses
2 teaspoons Worcestershire sauce
1 tablespoon extra-virgin olive oil
2 tablespoons red wine vinegar
1 teaspoon kosher salt
½ teaspoon coarsely ground black pepper

1. Combine the balsamic vinegar, garlic, and rosemary in a small saucepan and boil over high heat until reduced by half. Remove the rosemary sprigs and let the mixture cool to room temperature.

2. Put the roasted peppers, horseradish, honey, molasses, and Worcestershire in a blender, add the cooled balsamic mixture, the olive oil, and red wine vinegar, and blend until smooth; season with the salt and black pepper.

NACHO DOGS
(PAGE 196)

NEW YORK
STREET-
CART DOGS

If there ever were a true New York hot dog, this is it. In my hometown, we have a hot dog cart on every corner, and the city's topping of choice is a soft-cooked onion sauce, red from ketchup and slightly sweet and spicy with cinnamon and ancho chile. Another New York tradition? Little Italy's San Gennaro festival, where food vendors hawk sweet and spicy sausages topped with griddled bell peppers. This dog has a delicious sampling of both toppings. **SERVES 4 TO 8**

NEW YORK STREET-CART DOGS

||| WITH ||| *onion sauce* ||| AND |||

red pepper relish

1 Heat your grill to high for direct grilling (see page 23).

2 Make the red pepper relish: Brush the bell peppers with canola oil and grill, turning, until charred all over, about 10 minutes. Remove to a bowl, cover, and let sit for 10 minutes. Peel, seed, and thinly slice the peppers.

3 Combine the bell peppers, garlic, olive oil, vinegar, and chopped parsley in a bowl and season with salt and pepper. Cover and let sit at room temperature for at least 30 minutes before serving.

4 Make the onion sauce: Heat the oil in a medium saucepan over medium heat. Add the onions and cook until soft, 8 to 10 minutes. Stir in the ancho powder and cinnamon and cook for 1 minute. Add the ketchup, 1 cup water, the hot sauce, salt, and black pepper and bring to a simmer. Cook until thickened, 10 to 15 minutes. Transfer to a bowl and let cool to room temperature before serving.

5 Cook the hot dogs: Brush the dogs with oil and season with black pepper. Grill until slightly charred and golden brown on all sides, about 8 minutes.

6 Spread the bottoms of the bun with mustard, top with a hot dog, and top the dog with the onion sauce and then the red pepper relish. Garnish with parsley leaves.

RED PEPPER RELISH
3 red bell peppers
Canola oil
6 garlic cloves, roasted and coarsely chopped
3 tablespoons extra-virgin olive oil
1 tablespoon red wine vinegar
3 tablespoons finely chopped fresh flat-leaf parsley
Kosher salt and freshly ground black pepper

ONION SAUCE
2 tablespoons canola oil
2 large Spanish onions, halved and thinly sliced
1 teaspoon ancho chile powder
½ teaspoon ground cinnamon
¼ cup ketchup
¼ teaspoon hot sauce
½ teaspoon kosher salt
¼ teaspoon freshly ground black pepper

HOT DOGS
8 all-beef kosher hot dogs
Canola oil
Freshly ground black pepper
8 hot dog buns
Dijon mustard

Two of my favorite ballpark guilty pleasures come together into one dynamite dog: a plump and juicy hot dog, charred to perfection and topped with crunchy bits of tortilla chips, a smoky grilled tomato–chipotle salsa, smooth guacamole, and shredded cheese. It's indulgent, sure, but deliciously so. I served up this dog in a Throwdown against LA's legendary hot dog restaurant Pink's, and much to our surprise, it won. To those of you who are lucky enough to have been to Pink's, and are asking the question, I have to say yes, the nacho dog is that good.

SERVES 4 TO 8

GRILLED TOMATO-CHIPOTLE SALSA
4 plum tomatoes
4 tablespoons canola oil
Kosher salt and freshly ground black pepper
3 tablespoons red wine vinegar
2 teaspoons pureed canned chipotle in adobo
3 tablespoons finely diced red onion

HOT DOGS
8 kosher beef or turkey hot dogs
8 hot dog buns, opened
1½ cups grated Monterey Jack cheese
½ cup sliced pickled jalapeños
Guacamole (recipe follows)
Fried blue corn tortilla chips, coarsely crumbled
Fresh cilantro leaves, for garnish

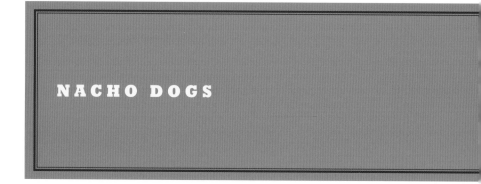

NACHO DOGS

1 Make the salsa: Heat your grill to high for direct grilling (see page 23).

2 Brush the tomatoes with 2 tablespoons of the oil and season with salt and pepper. Grill until charred on all sides, about 6 minutes. Remove the tomatoes from the grill. Slice in half, remove and discard the seeds, and coarsely chop.

3 Whisk together the remaining 2 tablespoons oil, the vinegar, chipotle puree, and red onion in a small bowl. Add the tomatoes and stir to combine; season with salt and pepper.

4 Cook the hot dogs: Grill the hot dogs until golden brown on all sides, about 7 minutes. Remove to a plate. Grill the buns, cut side down, until lightly golden brown, about 20 seconds.

5 Put the hot dogs in the buns and top with the Monterey Jack, jalapeños, guacamole, salsa, tortilla chips, and cilantro leaves.

GUACAMOLE
MAKES ABOUT 3 CUPS

GUACAMOLE

3 ripe Hass avocados, peeled, pitted, and
    coarsely chopped
1 large jalapeño, finely diced
¼ cup finely diced red onion
Juice of 1 lime
2 tablespoons canola oil
3 tablespoons chopped fresh cilantro
    leaves
Kosher salt and freshly ground black
    pepper

Combine the avocados, jalapeño, onion,
lime juice, oil, and cilantro in a bowl and
gently mix until combined; season with
salt and pepper.

I love a basic cheeseburger as much as—if not more than—the next guy, but I am also all about reinventing classics in new and exciting ways. This is a cheeseburger done up Louisiana style. Blackening, the Paul Prudhomme—mastered method of coating and searing a peppery crust on protein, is best done in a cast-iron pan. Salty, slightly spicy tasso ham and pepper Jack cheese add more New Orleans heat and flavor, and the city's favorite condiment, rémoulade, crowns the burger with style. **SERVES 4**

1 tablespoon mild Spanish paprika
1 teaspoon dried thyme
½ teaspoon garlic powder
½ teaspoon onion powder
½ teaspoon cayenne
Kosher salt and freshly ground black
   pepper
1½ pounds 80% lean ground chuck
1 tablespoon canola oil
8 thin slices pepper Jack cheese
4 slices tasso ham
4 soft sesame seed buns, split
Rémoulade Sauce (recipe follows)
4 slices red onion
2 tablespoons Frank's RedHot sauce

BLACKENED BURGERS ||| WITH |||
pepper jack ||| AND ||| *rèmoulade*

1 Heat your grill or griddle to high for direct grilling (see page 23).
2 Combine the paprika, thyme, garlic and onion powders, cayenne, 2 teaspoons salt, and 2 teaspoons black pepper in a small bowl.
3 Form the meat into 4 uniform, fairly flat patties, each no thicker than ¾ inch, and then make a deep depression in the center of each with your thumb. Brush on both sides with the oil. Season one side of each of the patties with the spice mixture, making sure to rub the spices into the meat.
4 Grill the burgers, spice rub side down, until slightly charred and the spices have formed a crust, about 2 minutes (be careful not to burn the spices). Season the top side with salt and pepper, turn over the

burgers so that they are over medium heat, and continue cooking to desired doneness, about 6 minutes for medium. During the last minute of cooking, put 2 slices of pepper Jack on each burger, cover the grill, and cook until the cheese has completely melted. Transfer the burgers to a warm platter.
5 Grill the ham until lightly browned and warmed through, about 30 seconds per side. Grill the buns, split side down, until toasted, about 20 seconds.
6 Spread some of the rémoulade sauce on the tops and bottoms of each bun, put a slice of red onion on each bottom bun, and top with a cheeseburger. Add the ham, drizzle the ham with some of the hot sauce, and finish with the bun tops.

RÉMOULADE SAUCE
MAKES ABOUT 1⅔ CUPS

½ cup mayonnaise
¼ cup Dijon mustard
¼ cup whole grain mustard
3 tablespoons Frank's RedHot sauce or
   your favorite hot sauce
3 cornichons, finely diced
2 green onions, green and pale green
   parts, finely diced
Kosher salt and freshly ground black
   pepper

Whisk together the mayonnaise, both mustards, the hot sauce, cornichons, and green onions in a small bowl and season with salt and pepper. Cover and refrigerate for at least 30 minutes before serving to allow the flavors to meld.

This burger is just all kinds of delicious. If you haven't spent much time in the South you may not be familiar with pimiento cheese, and if that's the case, it's high time you got to know this magical concoction. It's a simple mix of cheese, roasted peppers, and mayonnaise that comes together into one delightfully tasty spread for crackers, a simple sandwich filling, a dip for veggies, or a topping for a decadent burger like this one. **SERVES 4**

PIMIENTO CHEESE–BACON BURGERS

1 cup mayonnaise
Kosher salt and freshly ground black pepper
½ teaspoon cayenne
¾ pound extra sharp white cheddar cheese, coarsely grated
¾ pound extra sharp yellow cheddar cheese, coarsely grated
1 cup drained and finely diced, jarred roasted red bell peppers
1½ pounds 80% lean ground chuck
2 tablespoons canola oil
4 hamburger buns, split and toasted
8 slices double-smoked bacon, cooked until crisp
Fresh cilantro leaves

1 Whisk together the mayonnaise, ½ teaspoon salt, ½ teaspoon black pepper, and the cayenne in a large bowl. Add the cheddar cheeses and roasted peppers and gently fold until combined. Cover and refrigerate for at least 30 minutes.

2 Heat your grill to high for direct grilling (see page 23).

3 Form the meat into 4 uniform, fairly flat patties, each no thicker than ¾ inch, and then make a deep depression in the center of each with your thumb. Brush both sides with oil and season liberally with salt and black pepper. Grill until golden brown, slightly charred on both sides, and cooked to medium, about 4 minutes per side. During the last minute of cooking, spoon a dollop of the cheese mixture on top of each burger, close the cover, and cook until the cheese has just melted, about 1 minute.

4 Put the burgers on the buns and top each with 2 slices of bacon and some cilantro leaves.

OAXACA
BURGERS

PIMIENTO CHEESE-
BACON BURGERS
(PAGE 199)

Central Mexico's Oaxaca is home to a refined cuisine whose crowning glory is mole. Gathering the ingredients needed to prepare this rich sauce may take some effort, but the end result—smoky, earthy, with a delicate balance of fruity heat—is well worth it. Paired with nutty Manchego cheese, creamy avocado, and spicy, acidic onions, this sophisticated burger hits all the right notes. **SERVES 4**

OAXACA BURGERS

||| WITH ||| *manchego, avocado,* ||| AND ||| *pickled habanero onions*

recipe continues >>

MOLE

¼ cup slivered raw almonds

2 tablespoons canola oil

1 small Spanish onion, coarsely chopped

3 garlic cloves, coarsely chopped

1 cup pureed plum tomatoes

3 cups low-sodium chicken broth, plus more if needed

Scant ¼ cup pureed canned chipotle in adobo

2 tablespoons ancho chile powder

1 tablespoon New Mexican chile powder

½ teaspoon chile de árbol powder

¼ cup chopped mango

¼ cup golden raisins

¼ cup crushed blue corn tortilla chips

1 tablespoon clover honey

1 tablespoon pure grade B maple syrup

3 tablespoons molasses

¾ teaspoon ground cinnamon

½ teaspoon ground cloves

½ teaspoon ground allspice

1 ounce semisweet or bittersweet chocolate, finely chopped

Kosher salt and freshly ground black pepper

BURGERS

1½ pounds 80% lean ground chuck, or 90% lean ground turkey

2 tablespoons canola oil

Kosher salt and freshly ground black pepper

1 cup grated Manchego cheese

4 hamburger buns, split

Pickled Habanero Onions (recipe follows)

1 ripe Hass avocado, peeled, pitted, and sliced

1 Make the mole: Put the almonds in a medium saucepan over medium heat and toast, stirring occasionally, until lightly golden brown, about 5 minutes. Remove the almonds to a plate.

2 Increase the heat to high, add the oil to the saucepan, and heat until it begins to shimmer. Add the onion and cook until soft, about 4 minutes. Add the garlic and cook for 30 seconds. Stir in the tomatoes, chicken broth, chipotle, and chile powders. Bring to a boil and cook for 10 minutes.

3 Add the mango, raisins, tortilla chips, and almonds and cook, stirring occasionally, until the mango is soft and the mixture is reduced by half, about 20 minutes.

4 Carefully transfer the mixture to a blender and blend until smooth. Return the mixture to the pan over high heat. Add the honey, maple syrup, molasses, cinnamon, cloves, allspice, and chocolate, and cook until reduced to a sauce consistency, about 10 minutes; season with salt and pepper.

5 Heat your grill to high for direct grilling (see page 23).

6 Cook the burgers: Form the meat into 4 uniform, fairly flat patties, each no thicker than ¾ inch, and then make a deep depression in the center of each with your thumb. Brush the burgers on both sides with the oil and season with salt and pepper. Grill the burgers until golden brown, slightly charred on both sides, and cooked to medium, about 4 minutes per side. During the last minute of cooking, add the Manchego to the burgers, close the cover, and cook until the cheese has completely melted, about 1 minute.

7 Grill the buns, split side down, until toasted, about 20 seconds.

8 Remove the burgers to the buns and top each with a large dollop of the mole sauce, some of the pickled habanero onions, and avocado.

PICKLED HABANERO ONIONS
MAKES 1 CUP

¾ cup fresh lime juice
¾ cup distilled white vinegar
2 tablespoons superfine sugar
2 teaspoons kosher salt
½ habanero chile, seeds removed
1 large red onion, halved and cut into ⅛-inch-thick slices
2 teaspoons finely chopped fresh oregano
2 tablespoons finely chopped fresh cilantro leaves

1. Combine the lime juice, vinegar, ½ cup water, the sugar, salt, and habanero in a medium nonreactive saucepan. Bring to a boil and cook until the sugar is dissolved, about 2 minutes. Remove from the heat and let cool for 5 minutes.

2. Put the red onion slices in a small bowl. Pour in the warm vinegar mixture, add the oregano and cilantro, and toss to coat. Cover and refrigerate, stirring the mixture a few times, for at least 4 hours and up to 48 hours.

I'm a big fan of pairing fruit with meat. I just love to play sweet off of savory and this combination of lamb and apricot does just that. The glaze of apricot jam and balsamic vinegar couldn't be easier to make and is full of flavor. This dish is Turkish in inspiration—lamb, sweet-tart apricots, mild and nutty pistachios, and lemony sumac are all ingredients favored in Turkey and the Middle East. **SERVES 4**

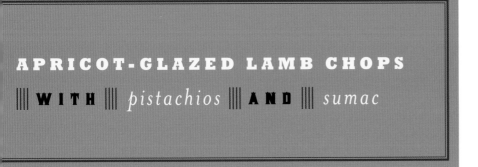

APRICOT-GLAZED LAMB CHOPS
||| WITH ||| *pistachios* ||| AND ||| *sumac*

8 (4- to 5-ounce) lamb porterhouse chops
¾ cup apricot jam
1 tablespoon balsamic vinegar
Kosher salt and freshly ground black pepper
2 tablespoons canola oil
¼ cup shelled pistachios, lightly toasted and coarsely chopped
1 teaspoon sumac
Fresh flat-leaf parsley leaves, for garnish

1 Remove the lamb from the refrigerator 30 minutes before cooking.
2 Heat your grill to high for direct grilling (see page 23).
3 Whisk together the jam and balsamic vinegar and season with salt and pepper.
4 Brush the chops with the oil on both sides and season with salt and pepper. Grill until golden brown and slightly charred, about 3 minutes. Flip over the chops, brush with some of the apricot glaze, and continue grilling, brushing with more of the glaze, until cooked to medium, about 3 minutes.
5 Remove the chops to a platter and sprinkle with the pistachios, sumac, and parsley.

Rich lamb, cold-smoked for extra flavor, is a perfect foil for the mild yet meaty black beans in these satisfying tacos. Tangy, creamy goat cheese and a peppery watercress vinaigrette complete the dish with bright flair. **SERVES 4 TO 8**

2 pounds lamb loin
3 tablespoons canola oil
Kosher salt and freshly ground black
    pepper
½ small red onion, finely diced
1 (15.5-ounce) can black beans, drained,
    rinsed, and drained again
1 teaspoon dried Mexican oregano
8 (6-inch) flour tortillas
1 cup grated Monterey Jack cheese
12 ounces fresh goat cheese, crumbled
Watercress Vinaigrette (recipe follows)
1 bunch watercress
Hot sauce

COLD-SMOKED LAMB LOIN
||| AND ||| BLACK BEAN TACOS
||| WITH ||| *watercress vinaigrette*

1 Soak 1 cup of mesquite wood chips for 30 minutes.

2 Heat your grill to very low for indirect grilling (see page 23).

3 If using a charcoal grill, scatter the drained wood chips over the coals. If the temperature in the grill is hotter than 100°F, put 2 cups of ice cubes in an aluminum tray and nestle the tray next to the coals on the bottom grate. Put the cooking grate in place. If using a gas grill, put the drained wood chips in a smoker box. Add a tray of ice cubes, if needed, to the cooking grate. Then, for either grill, close the cover and let smoke build until the temperature in the grill reaches 100°F.

4 Arrange the lamb in a single layer on the grill. Open the top vent slightly and close the cover so that the smoke stays inside. Cold-smoke the lamb for 15 minutes. Remove from the grill.

5 Heat your grill to high for direct grilling (see page 23).

6 Brush the lamb with 2 tablespoons of the oil and season with salt and pepper. Grill until charred on all sides and cooked to medium-rare, 10 to 12 minutes. Remove the lamb to a cutting board, tent loosely with foil, and let rest for 10 minutes before slicing thinly.

7 Heat 1 tablespoon of the remaining oil in a medium sauté pan until it begins to shimmer. Add the red onion and cook until soft, about 5 minutes. Add the beans, ½ cup water, and oregano and cook until heated through and softened, about 10 minutes.

8 Grill the tortillas for 10 seconds on each side. Lay the tortillas on plates, top with some beans, and divide the cheeses over the beans. Add a few slices of lamb, drizzle with some of the watercress vinaigrette, and top with watercress. Drizzle with hot sauce to taste.

WATERCRESS VINAIGRETTE

MAKES ABOUT 1½ CUPS

3 tablespoons rice vinegar
1 tablespoon fresh lime juice
1 garlic clove, chopped
2 teaspoons Dijon mustard
Kosher salt and freshly ground
      black pepper
1 cup packed watercress leaves
¼ cup sliced green onions, green
      and pale green parts
½ cup extra-virgin olive oil
Clover honey

Combine the vinegar, lime juice, garlic, and mustard in a blender and pulse a few times to blend. Season with salt and pepper. Add the watercress, green onions, and a splash of water and blend until smooth. With the motor running, slowly add the oil and blend until emulsified. Add honey to taste and blend to combine.

This quesadilla is the perfect platform for some big flavors. Lamb stands up well to the full, complex mole rub; the two are a classic pairing. The ancho-cherry jam offers a tingle of fruity heat, while tangy goat cheese crema cools it all down.

SERVES 8

MOLE-RUBBED LAMB TENDERLOIN QUESADILLAS
||| WITH ||| *ancho-cherry jam*

3 tablespoons ancho chile powder
1 tablespoon New Mexican chile powder
½ teaspoon chile de árbol powder
2 teaspoons unsweetened cocoa powder
1 teaspoon packed light brown sugar
1 teaspoon ground cinnamon
¼ teaspoon ground allspice
¼ teaspoon ground cloves
Kosher salt and freshly ground black pepper
1¼ pounds lamb tenderloin, trimmed of extra fat
4 ounces fresh goat cheese, crumbled
½ cup crema, crème fraîche, or sour cream
Canola oil
12 (6-inch) white corn tortillas
1½ cups grated white cheddar cheese
Ancho-Cherry Jam (recipe follows)
Chopped fresh flat-leaf parsley, for garnish

1 Combine the chile powders, cocoa powder, brown sugar, cinnamon, allspice, cloves, 1 teaspoon salt, and ¼ teaspoon pepper in a small bowl. Rub each tenderloin with some of the mole rub and let sit at room temperature for 30 minutes.

2 Heat your grill to high for direct grilling (see page 23).

3 Stir together the goat cheese and crema and season with salt and pepper. Cover and refrigerate until ready to use.

4 Drizzle the lamb with oil and grill until golden brown on both sides and cooked to medium-rare, about 2 to 3 minutes per side. Remove the lamb to a cutting board, tent loosely with foil, and let rest for 10 minutes.

5 Put 8 of the tortillas on a flat surface. Divide the cheddar cheese over the tortillas and season each layer with salt and pepper.

6 Stack the tortillas to make four 2-layer tortillas and top each with 1 of the remaining 4 tortillas. Brush the tops of the tortillas with oil. Carefully place the quesadillas on the grill, oil side down, and grill until golden brown, about 1 minute. Brush the tops with oil and turn the quesadillas over. Close the cover and grill until the bottoms are golden brown, about 1 minute. Transfer the quesadillas to a baking sheet, put the baking sheet on the grill, close the cover, and cook until the cheese has melted, about 5 minutes.

7 Cut the quesadillas into quarters and top with ancho-cherry jam, goat cheese crema, lamb, and chopped parsley.

recipe continues >>

ANCHO-CHERRY JAM
MAKES 1 CUP

2 dried ancho chiles, stemmed and
    seeded
2 tablespoons canola oil
1 small red onion, finely diced
2 tablespoons finely grated fresh ginger
2 garlic cloves, finely chopped
½ cup fresh orange juice
3 tablespoons packed light brown sugar
1 tablespoon clover honey
1 pound fresh sweet red cherries, pitted
    and halved
¼ cup chopped fresh cilantro leaves

1. Soak the ancho chiles in 2 cups hot water
for 30 minutes. Remove from the soaking
liquid, reserving the liquid. Transfer the
chiles to a food processor with ½ cup of the
soaking liquid and process until smooth.
2. Heat the oil in a medium saucepan over
medium heat. Add the onion and cook until
soft, about 5 minutes. Add the ginger and
garlic and cook for 30 seconds. Add the
orange juice, ¼ cup of the ancho soaking
liquid, the brown sugar, and honey and stir
until the brown sugar is dissolved, about
2 minutes. Stir in the cherries and ancho
puree and cook until the cherries soften
and begin to break down and the mixture
thickens, 20 to 30 minutes.
3. Transfer the jam to a bowl, stir in the
cilantro, and let cool to room temperature.

I highly recommend that you seek out the fennel pollen that I call for in the rub for these lamb chops. While you can substitute toasted and ground fennel seeds in a pinch, fennel pollen has an incredible sweet intensity and smooth anise flavor that can't quite be matched. Once a treasured secret of the northern Italians, fennel pollen has been making its way into the American culinary lexicon since the mid-1990s and is becoming more and more available to the home cook via websites such as www.thespicehouse.com. It adds such richness to tender baby lamb chops. A briny green olive tapenade, given an unexpected touch of fresh heat from jalapeño, completes the dish with vibrancy. **SERVES 4**

FENNEL-RUBBED BABY LAMB CHOPS ║ WITH ║ *spicy green olive tapenade*

GREEN OLIVE TAPENADE

2 cups assorted green olives, pitted
¼ cup slivered almonds, lightly toasted, plus more for garnish
2 anchovy fillets, patted dry
1 tablespoon brined capers, drained
1 garlic clove, chopped
1 jalapeño, diced
1 teaspoon grated lemon zest
Juice of ½ lemon
½ cup extra-virgin olive oil, plus more for drizzling
¼ cup fresh flat-leaf parsley leaves, plus more for garnish
Kosher salt and freshly ground black pepper

LAMB

12 baby (3-ounce) frenched lamb chops
2 tablespoons canola oil
Kosher salt
2 tablespoons fennel pollen or 1½ tablespoons fennel seeds, lightly toasted and ground

1 Make the tapenade: Combine the olives, almonds, anchovies, capers, garlic, jalapeño, lemon zest, and lemon juice in a food processor and process until coarsely chopped. With the motor running, slowly add the olive oil and process until emulsified. Add the parsley, season with salt and pepper, and pulse until the parsley is just incorporated, with specks of green still visible. Scrape into a bowl. (The tapenade can be stored, covered in the refrigerator, for up to 8 hours. Serve at room temperature.)

2 Prepare the lamb: Remove the lamb from the refrigerator 30 minutes before cooking.

3 Heat your grill to high for direct grilling (see page 23).

4 Brush the chops on both sides with canola oil and season with salt; season one side with the fennel. Grill, fennel side down, until golden brown and slightly charred, about 3 minutes. Flip over the chops and continue grilling until the bottoms are golden brown and slightly charred and the chops are cooked to medium-rare, about 2 minutes.

5 Remove the chops to a platter, top each with some of the tapenade, and garnish with almonds, parsley, and a drizzle of olive oil.

The sauce here is a little bit sweet, a little savory, a little spicy, a little smoky, and totally delicious. Known in the Middle East as muhammara, *it is a deep-hued spread of roasted red peppers, walnuts, garlic, and pomegranate molasses. Slathered on a richly spiced lamb patty and sandwiched with sweet grilled onions and salty Kasseri cheese between freshly grilled pizza dough, this is a patty melt extraordinaire.*

SERVES 4

½ cup finely chopped fresh flat-leaf parsley leaves

⅓ cup whole milk Greek yogurt

3 garlic cloves, finely chopped

2 teaspoons ground coriander

½ teaspoon ground cumin

½ teaspoon smoked mild paprika

¼ teaspoon ground allspice

Kosher salt and freshly ground black pepper

1¼ pounds ground lamb

1½ pounds pizza dough, homemade (page 61) or store-bought

Canola oil

1 pound aged Kasseri cheese, grated

1 large Vidalia onion, thinly sliced

Red Pepper–Walnut Sauce (recipe follows)

LAMB PATTY MELTS
||| **WITH** ||| *red pepper—walnut*
sauce ||| **AND** ||| *grilled onions*

1 Heat a grill to medium-high for indirect grilling (see page 23).

2 Combine the parsley, yogurt, garlic, coriander, cumin, paprika, allspice, 1 teaspoon salt, and ¼ teaspoon pepper in a large bowl. Add the lamb and mix gently by hand until evenly combined. Form the meat into 4 uniform, fairly flat patties, each no thicker than ¾ inch, and then make a deep depression in the center of each with your thumb.

3 Divide the dough into quarters and roll each piece into a 12 x 5-inch rectangle. Oil one side of each piece of dough very lightly. Grill the dough, oiled side down, over medium-high heat until the bottom is charred, about 1 minute. Lightly oil the top and flip over the dough. Scatter the Kasseri over the dough and cook until the underside is charred, about 1 minute. Move to the cooler side of the grill (indirect heat), close the cover, and cook until the cheese is melted and the dough is cooked through, 3 to 5 minutes. Remove the rectangle from the grill. Cut each rectangle in half crosswise and keep warm while you grill the burgers.

4 Brush the patties on both sides with oil and arrange on the hot side of the grill. Cook for 3 to 4 minutes, flip the patties, and grill for another 2 to 3 minutes for medium-rare to medium.

RED PEPPER–WALNUT SAUCE
MAKES 1¼ CUPS

3 grilled or jarred roasted large red bell
   peppers, peeled, seeded, and chopped
1 serrano chile, grilled, peeled, seeded,
   and roughly chopped (see page 122)
1 cup walnut pieces, toasted
1 garlic clove, chopped
1 teaspoon ground cumin
½ teaspoon smoked mild paprika
2 tablespoons extra-virgin olive oil, or
   more if needed
1 tablespoon pomegranate molasses
1 tablespoon sherry vinegar
Grated zest and juice of ½ lemon
Kosher salt
⅛ teaspoon cayenne, optional

Put the roasted peppers, serrano, walnuts,
garlic, cumin, paprika, olive oil, molasses,
vinegar, and lemon juice in a food processor and process to a smooth paste; if the
mixture is too thick, drizzle in a little more
olive oil. Stir in the lemon zest by hand.
Season with salt and cayenne, if desired.

5 Meanwhile, brush the onion slices with
oil, season with salt and pepper, and grill
over medium-high heat until slightly charred
and softened, about 3 to 4 minutes per side.
6 Transfer the burgers to one half of each
rectangle, spread with some red pepper–
walnut sauce and grilled onions, and top
with the other halves of the grilled pizza
dough. Put the sandwiches back on the
grill over low heat for a few seconds per
side. Remove them from the grill, halve the
sandwiches on a long diagonal, and serve
immediately.

FISH AND SHELL

FISH

The Pacific Northwest is understandably known for its outstanding salmon, but Washington State and Oregon are also among the country's leading producers of apples, cherries, and hazelnuts—hence the pairing of this nutty apple and cherry salad with hot-smoked salmon. The full-flavored acidity of apple cider vinegar highlights the sweet-tart combination of Granny Smith and Gala apples as well as the dried cherries; the vinaigrette really helps cut the richness of the salmon.

SERVES 6 TO 8

HOT-SMOKED SALMON
||| WITH ||| *apples, dried cherries,* *hazelnuts,* ||| AND ||| *greens*

SALMON
½ cup kosher salt

2 tablespoons granulated sugar

2 tablespoons packed light brown sugar

2 teaspoons crushed black peppercorns

1 (3- to 3½-pound) piece center-cut salmon fillet, skin on, pin bones removed

SALAD
¼ cup apple cider vinegar

1 tablespoon whole-grain mustard

2 teaspoons clover honey

Kosher salt and freshly ground black pepper

¼ cup canola oil

4 ounces organic baby greens

1 Granny Smith apple, cored and thinly sliced

½ small white onion, halved and thinly sliced

¼ cup dried cherries

¼ cup chopped hazelnuts, toasted

recipe continues >>

1 **Cure the salmon:** Mix together the salt, granulated sugar, brown sugar, and peppercorns in a medium bowl. Line a piece of extra-wide aluminum foil that's a little longer than the length of the fish with an equally long layer of plastic wrap. Sprinkle half of the salt rub on the wrap. Lay the salmon on the rub. Sprinkle the remaining rub on top of the salmon. Cover with plastic and wrap in foil, crimping the edges together tightly around the fish. Put the wrapped fish on a rimmed baking sheet and top with another baking sheet. Weight with a brick or two and refrigerate for 24 hours.

2 Unwrap the salmon and rinse off the cure mixture with cold water. Pat dry with paper towels and put the salmon in a cool, dry place (not the refrigerator) until the surface of the fish is dry and somewhat matte, 1 to 3 hours, depending on humidity. A fan may be used to speed the process.

3 Soak 2 cups alder wood chips in water for at least 30 minutes.

4 Heat your smoker according to the manufacturer's instructions. If using a charcoal or gas grill, set up a drip pan with water on the bottom grates and heat the grill to low for indirect grilling (see page 23). For a charcoal grill, put the drained wood chips over the hot coals, add the cooking grate, and close the cover. For a gas grill, add the wood chips to a smoker box or foil pouch, put on the cooking grates toward the back, and close the cover. For both grills, open the vents halfway and maintain a temperature of 200°F. Let smoke build for 10 minutes.

5 Add the salmon to the smoker, skin side down, and cover the smoker. Adjust the heat as needed to maintain the temperature and smoke until the thickest part of the fish registers 150°F, about 1 hour. Serve immediately or cool to room temperature, wrap tightly in plastic, and refrigerate for up to 3 days.

6 **Make the salad:** Whisk together the vinegar, mustard, and honey in a large bowl and season with salt and pepper. Slowly whisk in the oil until emulsified. Add the greens, apple, onion, cherries, and hazelnuts and toss to combine. Season with salt and pepper.

7 Put the salmon on a platter and arrange the salad on top.

In a methodology that seems a bit reverse from what we're used to, the fish here is cooked and then marinated. Flaky mahimahi is simply grilled before taking a bath in a tart yet sweet mixture of grapefruit juice, vinegar, and honey. The vinegar almost pickles the vegetables in the marinade while diced avocado adds richness, jalapeño a touch of fresh heat, and mango tropical flair to this gorgeous dish.

SERVES 4

GRILLED ||| AND ||| MARINATED MAHIMAHI ||| WITH ||| *grapefruit, avocado,* ||| AND ||| *mango*

½ cup fresh ruby red grapefruit juice
2 tablespoons red wine vinegar
2 tablespoons clover honey
1 small Spanish onion, halved and thinly sliced
1 large jalapeño, thinly sliced
1 Hass avocado, pitted, peeled, and diced
1 small ripe mango, pitted, peeled, and diced
¼ cup extra-virgin olive oil
Kosher salt and freshly ground black pepper
4 (6-ounce) mahimahi fillets
Canola oil
¼ cup fresh cilantro leaves, plus more for garnish

1 Heat your grill to high for direct grilling (see page 23).

2 Whisk together the grapefruit juice, vinegar, and honey in a medium bowl. Stir in the onion, jalapeño, avocado, mango, and olive oil and season with salt and pepper. Let sit at room temperature while you grill the fish.

3 Brush the mahimahi on both sides with canola oil and season with salt and pepper. Grill until charred on both sides and almost cooked through, about 3 minutes per side. Put the fish on a platter. Add the cilantro leaves to the avocado mixture and then top the fish with the mixture. Let sit at room temperature for 30 minutes before serving to allow the flavors to meld and the acid to finish cooking the fish.

4 Garnish with cilantro leaves before serving.

Full flavored and rich in taste and texture, salmon pairs perfectly with this robustly smoky tomato chutney. The salmon is marinated in an earthy blend of Southwestern spices for tons of flavor. Crema (sour cream works, too) in the marinade imparts a touch of tanginess and an extra-silky texture. **SERVES 4**

SOUTHWESTERN MARINATED GRILLED SALMON ||| WITH |||
tomato—red chile chutney

1 cup crema, crème fraîche, or sour cream

3 garlic cloves, finely chopped

2 teaspoons grated lime zest

2 tablespoons fresh lime juice

1 heaping tablespoon ancho chile powder

2 teaspoons ground coriander

1 teaspoon ground cumin

¼ teaspoon ground turmeric

¼ teaspoon chile de árbol powder

4 (8-ounce) skin-on salmon fillets

2 tablespoons plus 1 teaspoon canola oil

Kosher salt and freshly ground black pepper

Chopped green onion, for garnish

2 limes, halved

Tomato—Red Chile Chutney (recipe follows)

1 Whisk together the crema, garlic, lime zest, lime juice, ancho powder, coriander, cumin, turmeric, and chile de árbol powder in a baking dish. Add the salmon fillets and turn to coat in the marinade. Cover and refrigerate for at least 20 minutes and up to 1 hour.

2 Heat your grill to high for direct grilling (see page 23).

3 Remove the salmon from the marinade and wipe off the excess with paper towels. Brush the salmon on both sides with 2 tablespoons of the oil and season with salt and pepper. Grill until golden brown on both sides and cooked to medium, about 4 minutes per side.

4 Meanwhile, brush the cut side of the limes with the remaining 1 teaspoon oil and put on the grill, cut side down, until browned, 1 minute.

5 Transfer the salmon to plates and garnish with green onion. Add a lime half onto each plate for squeezing over the salmon and serve the chutney on the side.

TOMATO–RED CHILE CHUTNEY
MAKES ABOUT 2 CUPS

2 dried ancho or New Mexican red chiles
2 tablespoons canola oil
1 small red onion, finely diced
1 garlic clove, finely chopped
4 plum tomatoes, halved and diced
1 teaspoon dried Mexican oregano
2 teaspoons clover honey
Kosher salt and freshly ground black
    pepper
3 green onions, green and pale green
    parts, finely diced

1. Soak the red chiles in 2 cups hot water for 30 minutes. Drain, reserving ¼ cup of the soaking liquid, and then stem, seed, and dice the chiles. Combine the chiles and the reserved soaking liquid in a blender and blend until smooth.
2. Heat the oil in a medium saucepan over medium heat. Add the red onion and cook until soft, about 5 minutes. Add the garlic and cook for 30 seconds. Add the red chile puree, bring to a boil, and cook until slightly thickened, about 5 minutes.

3. Add the tomatoes and oregano and cook until slightly softened, about 10 minutes. Stir in the honey and season with salt and pepper. Remove the chutney from the heat and fold in the green onions. Serve warm or at room temperature.

What many people don't realize is that there is not one curry spice, but rather a personalized mixture of spices that comes together as curry powder. The curry that flavors this silky sauce is not quite traditional; I like to throw in some ancho chile and chile de árbol powders for a touch of smoky heat. This curry sauce walks a careful line between sweet and savory, from the apple and the onion in the first stages of the sauce on down. That delicate balance is carried through in the chutney, which is like a cooked Indian salsa. **SERVES 4**

GRILLED HALIBUT ||| WITH |||

corn-coconut curry sauce

||| AND ||| *grilled cherry tomato chutney*

4 tablespoons canola oil, plus more for brushing
1 small Spanish onion, finely diced
½ small Granny Smith apple, cored and diced
2 garlic cloves, finely chopped
1½ tablespoons ancho chile powder
1 teaspoon ground cumin
1 teaspoon ground coriander
1 teaspoon ground fennel
1 teaspoon ground turmeric
½ teaspoon ground cardamom
½ teaspoon ground cloves
½ teaspoon chile de árbol powder
½ teaspoon freshly ground
    black pepper, plus more to taste

2 cups fish stock or vegetable stock
1 cup fresh or frozen corn kernels
1 cup unsweetened coconut milk
Clover honey
Kosher salt
3 tablespoons chopped fresh cilantro leaves
4 (6-ounce) skinless halibut fillets
Grilled Cherry Tomato Chutney (recipe follows)

recipe continues >>

1 Heat your grill to high for direct grilling (see page 23).

2 Heat 2 tablespoons of the oil in a medium sauté pan over high heat. Add the onion and apple and cook, stirring occasionally, until soft, about 5 minutes. Add the garlic and cook for 30 seconds. Add the ancho powder, cumin, coriander, fennel, turmeric, cardamom, cloves, chile de árbol powder, and pepper and cook for 2 minutes. Add the fish stock, bring to a boil, and cook for 10 minutes. Strain the curried stock into a bowl and discard the solids.

3 Heat the remaining 2 tablespoons oil in a large high-sided sauté pan. Add the corn and cook until golden brown. Add the curried stock and coconut milk and bring to a simmer. Cook until reduced and slightly thickened and the corn is tender, about 15 minutes. Season the sauce with honey, salt, and pepper and stir in the chopped cilantro. Keep warm.

4 Brush the halibut with oil on both sides and season with salt and pepper. Grill until slightly charred and just cooked through, about 4 minutes per side.

5 Ladle some of the sauce onto a platter, top with the fillets, and spoon tomato chutney over the fish.

GRILLED CHERRY TOMATO CHUTNEY

MAKES 2½ CUPS

1 pint cherry tomatoes
Canola oil
Kosher salt and freshly ground black pepper
2 green onions, green and white parts, thinly sliced
3 garlic cloves, finely chopped
2 tablespoons packed light brown sugar
¼ cup apple cider vinegar
⅛ teaspoon coriander seeds
⅛ teaspoon cumin seeds
⅛ teaspoon yellow mustard seeds

1. Heat your grill to high for direct grilling (see page 23).
2. Brush the tomatoes with oil, season with salt and pepper, and grill until charred and slightly soft, about 5 minutes.
3. Heat 2 tablespoons oil in a large sauté pan over high heat. Add the white and pale green parts of the green onions and the garlic and cook until soft, about 1 minute. Add the brown sugar, vinegar, ¼ cup water, the coriander seeds, cumin seeds, and mustard seeds and cook for 30 seconds. Add the tomatoes and cook for 2 minutes; season with salt and pepper. Fold in the dark green parts of the green onions. Let cool to room temperature.

I serve a version of this dish at my restaurant Bar Americain and was inspired to do so after a delicious trip to a rainbow trout farm in Ashville, North Carolina. You don't often think cool and refreshing when firing up the smoker, but this dish is just that. Bright, slightly sweet yet tart Meyer lemon dressing makes this a lighter take on a luncheon treat. **SERVES 4 TO 6**

SMOKED TROUT LETTUCE WRAPS ⫴ WITH ⫴ *meyer lemon dressing* ⫴ AND ⫴ *carrots*

Kosher salt and freshly ground black pepper
2 tablespoons packed light brown sugar
8 (6- to 8-ounce) trout fillets
½ teaspoon finely grated lemon zest
¼ cup freshly squeezed Meyer lemon juice or 3 tablespoons freshly squeezed lemon juice plus
1 tablespoon freshly squeezed orange juice
1 tablespoon red wine vinegar
2 tablespoons mayonnaise
1 heaping tablespoon whole grain mustard
2 teaspoons clover honey
½ cup extra-virgin olive oil
1 head butter lettuce, separated into leaves
2 medium carrots, julienned
Fresh flat-leaf parsley leaves, for garnish

1 Brine, dry, and smoke the trout fillets as on page 226. Remove the flesh from the skin and bones and flake into medium pieces.

2 Whisk together the lemon zest, lemon juice, vinegar, mayonnaise, mustard, and honey in a medium bowl. Season with salt and pepper, and then slowly whisk in the oil until emulsified.

3 Put several pieces of the trout in each lettuce leaf and drizzle with some of the dressing. Top with carrots and parsley leaves, roll, and eat.

This substantial salad is German in inspiration. Smoked trout is very popular in Germany, especially in the northern states of the country that border the Baltic and North Seas. I agree with the Germans—I find trout, with its full flavor, even texture, and manageable size, to be perfect for hot-smoking, and the end result is delicious. Germans also love their potatoes, and the creamy flesh and slightly charred exterior of fingerlings are a mild match for the smoky fish. The assertive vinaigrette is once again an homage to typically German flavors, full of the dill, horseradish, apple cider vinegar, and mustard they love in pickles and condiments. Use a smoker or charcoal (not gas) grill for this recipe. **SERVES 8**

Kosher salt and freshly ground black pepper

2 tablespoons packed light brown sugar

8 (6- to 8-ounce) trout fillets

2 pounds fingerling potatoes, parboiled in salted water, drained, and halved

3 tablespoons canola oil

1 teaspoon smoked mild paprika

¼ cup mayonnaise

¼ cup apple cider vinegar

2 tablespoons prepared horseradish

2 tablespoons whole grain mustard

¼ cup chopped fresh dill, plus whole dill sprigs for garnish

1 English cucumber, sliced

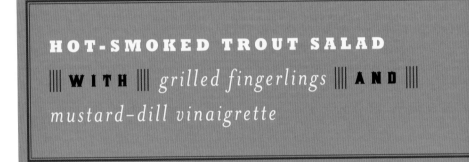

HOT-SMOKED TROUT SALAD
WITH *grilled fingerlings* AND
mustard–dill vinaigrette

1 Combine 1 quart water, ½ cup salt, and the brown sugar in a saucepan. Bring to a boil and cook to dissolve the salt and sugar, about 5 minutes. Remove from the heat and let cool completely.

2 Add the trout fillets to the brine, making sure they are submerged. Cover and refrigerate for at least 1 hour and up to 3 hours.

3 Remove the trout from the brine, rinse thoroughly with cold water, and pat dry with paper towels. Put the trout, skin side down, on a rack set over a baking sheet. Refrigerate for 21 to 24 hours or until the skin becomes shiny and somewhat tacky to the touch.

4 Soak 1 cup alder or apple wood chips in water for at least 30 minutes.

5 Heat your smoker according to the manufacturer's instructions. If using a charcoal grill, set up a drip pan with water on the bottom grates and heat the grill to low for indirect grilling (see page 23). Put half of the drained wood chips over the hot coals, add the cooking grate, and close the cover. Open the vents halfway and maintain a temperature of 150°F to 160°F. Let smoke build for 10 minutes.

6 Put the trout on the grill, skin side down, separating the fillets by at least ¼ inch, and close the cover. Adjust the heat as needed to maintain the temperature, add drained wood chips and hot coals as needed, and add more water to the drip pan if needed. Smoke until the fish is cooked through, has darkened in color, and has the desired level of smoke, 2 to 3 hours. Serve immediately or cool to room temperature, wrap tightly in plastic wrap, and refrigerate for up to 3 days. Remove the

flesh from the skin and bones and flake into medium pieces before serving.

7 Heat your smoker or grill to high for direct grilling (see page 23).

8 Toss the potatoes with the oil and paprika and season with salt and pepper. Transfer to a grill basket and grill, tossing occasionally, until golden brown and cooked through, about 10 minutes.

9 Meanwhile, whisk together the mayonnaise, vinegar, horseradish, mustard, and chopped dill and season with salt and pepper.

10 Drizzle some of the dressing over the bottom of a large serving platter. Pour the warm potatoes onto the platter and scatter the smoked trout on top. Add the cucumber and dill sprigs and drizzle with more dressing.

New England fishermen search high and low in their quest for this meaty fish, so showing it some love is the very least we can do. Too often it is overcooked and, as a result, dry. Smoking not only infuses the fish with rich flavor, it also gives it a meltingly moist texture. A sauce of white clams, bright with fresh parsley and pungent garlic, enhances the dish with its brininess. **SERVES 4**

HOT-SMOKED SWORDFISH
WITH *white clam, garlic,* **AND** *parsley sauce*

SWORDFISH
1 cup kosher salt, plus more to taste
¾ cup sugar
2 tablespoons black peppercorns
1 (2-pound) chunk skinless swordfish loin, 4 inches thick
2 to 3 tablespoons canola oil
Freshly ground black pepper

CLAM SAUCE
1 tablespoon canola oil
3 garlic cloves, finely chopped
1 serrano chile, finely diced
1 cup dry white wine
1¼ pounds littleneck clams or cockles in the shell, soaked in water and scrubbed
½ pound chopped shucked littleneck clams or cockles, and their juices

2 tablespoons unsalted butter, cold, cut into pieces
3 tablespoons finely chopped fresh flat-leaf parsley leaves, plus more leaves for garnish
2 teaspoons finely chopped fresh oregano
Grated zest of 1 lemon
Kosher salt and freshly ground black pepper

recipe continues >>

1 **Brine the swordfish:** Bring 2 quarts cold water, the salt, sugar, and peppercorns to a boil in a pot and cook until the salt and sugar dissolve. Remove from the heat and let cool completely.

2 Submerge the swordfish in the cool brine, cover, and refrigerate for 12 hours.

3 Remove the swordfish from the brine and rinse well under cold water. Pat dry with paper towels and allow to air-dry for at least 1 hour. The exterior of the fish should feel sticky to the touch before smoking.

4 Soak 1 to 2 cups maple wood chips in water for at least 30 minutes.

5 Heat your smoker according to the manufacturer's instructions. If using a charcoal or gas grill, set up a drip pan with water on the bottom grates and heat the grill to low for indirect grilling (see page 23). For a charcoal grill, put half of the drained wood chips over the hot coals, add the cooking grate, and close the cover. For a gas grill, add the wood chips to a smoker box or foil pouch, put on the cooking grates toward the back, and close the cover. For both grills, open the vents halfway and maintain a temperature between 200°F and 225°F. Let smoke build for 10 minutes.

6 Brush the swordfish very lightly with oil and season with salt and ground pepper. Put the fish in the smoker or grill and close the cover. Smoke until the fish is opaque, flakes easily when prodded with a fork, and reaches an internal temperature of 145°F, 1½ to 2 hours. Adjust the heat as needed to maintain the temperature and smoke, adding hot coals as needed and water to the drip pan. Add an additional cup of drained wood chips during the second hour if you prefer a much smokier flavor.

7 **Make the clam sauce:** Heat the oil in a medium saucepan over high heat. Add the garlic and serrano and cook for a few seconds. Pour in the white wine and bring to a simmer. Add the clams in their shells, stir, cover the pan, and cook until the clams open, about 5 minutes. Use a slotted spoon to remove the clams to a large bowl and set aside. Discard any that did not open.

8 Add the chopped clams to the pan and cook for 2 minutes. Stir in the butter. Remove from the heat and stir in the parsley, oregano, and lemon zest; season with salt and pepper.

9 Transfer the smoked swordfish to a large platter and pour the clam sauce over and around the fish. Garnish with the whole clams and parsley leaves.

Kofte, which are Middle Eastern spiced meatballs, are most commonly made with lamb or beef. I wanted to try something a little lighter with these, yet with enough heft to stand up to the full-flavored glaze and the heady spices in the kofte themselves. Making these with freshly diced tuna in place of ground meat was the perfect answer. Meaty tuna holds its own in both flavor and texture and doesn't pale when paired with rich spices and this glorious sweet-tart glaze. The spicy hummus, which lends a creamy, rich touch to the dish, is also a fantastic recipe on its own. You'll want to scoop it up with pita wedges, serve it as a dip for crudités, smear it on sandwiches . . . you get the picture. **SERVES 4**

TUNA KOFTE ||| WITH ||| *pomegranate molasses—mint glaze* ||| AND ||| *crushed spicy hummus*

POMEGRANATE MOLASSES—MINT GLAZE
½ cup pomegranate molasses
1 tablespoon clover honey
2 teaspoons fresh lemon juice
2 teaspoons Dijon mustard
8 fresh mint leaves, finely chopped
Kosher salt and freshly ground black pepper

TUNA KOFTE
1½ pounds fresh tuna
5 tablespoons canola oil
1 small red onion, finely grated or diced
2 garlic cloves, smashed to a paste
3 tablespoons tomato paste
1 teaspoon ground cumin
½ teaspoon ground cinnamon
½ teaspoon ground allspice
⅛ teaspoon cayenne

¼ cup finely chopped fresh flat-leaf parsley leaves
Grated zest and juice of 1 lemon
Kosher salt and freshly ground black pepper
Flatbread, homemade (page 65) or store-bought, for serving
Crushed Spicy Hummus (recipe follows)
Fresh mint leaves, torn

recipe continues >>

1 Make the glaze: Whisk together the molasses, honey, lemon juice, mustard, and mint and season with salt and pepper. Let the mixture sit at room temperature for at least 30 minutes before using.

2 Prepare the tuna: Put ¾ pound of the tuna in a food processor and process until coarsely chopped. Transfer to a large bowl. Finely dice the remaining tuna and add to the bowl. Keep cold.

3 Heat 2 tablespoons of the oil in a small sauté pan over high heat. Add the red onion and cook until soft, about 5 minutes. Add the garlic and cook for 30 seconds. Add the tomato paste, cumin, cinnamon, allspice, and cayenne and cook for 1 minute. Add ¾ cup water, bring to a boil, and cook until reduced slightly, about 2 minutes. Remove from the heat and let cool slightly.

4 Add the cooled spice mixture, the parsley, lemon zest, and lemon juice to the tuna and mix to combine. Season with salt and pepper. Divide the mixture into 12 equal portions and roll into small footballs. Put on a baking sheet, cover loosely with plastic wrap, and chill in the refrigerator for at least 30 minutes.

5 Heat a grill to high for direct grilling (see page 23). If using wood skewers, soak them in cold water for at least 15 minutes.

6 Skewer the koftes, then brush with the remaining 3 tablespoons oil and season with salt and pepper. Grill on all sides until golden brown, slightly charred, and just cooked through, about 6 minutes. Brush with some of the glaze.

7 Meanwhile, grill the bread quickly, about 20 seconds per side.

8 Divide the kofte among 4 plates, garnish with mint, and serve the flatbread and hummus on the side.

CRUSHED SPICY HUMMUS
MAKES ABOUT 2 CUPS

1 tablespoon canola oil
4 garlic cloves, chopped
1 serrano chile, finely diced
2 (15.5-ounce) cans chickpeas, drained, rinsed well, and drained again
Grated zest and juice of 1 lemon
¼ cup tahini
2 teaspoons toasted sesame oil
Few dashes of Tabasco sauce
½ cup extra-virgin olive oil
Kosher salt and freshly ground black pepper

1. Heat the canola oil in a medium saucepan over medium heat. Add the garlic and serrano and cook until soft, about 1 minute. Stir in the chickpeas and cook until just heated through, about 2 minutes.
2. Add the lemon zest, lemon juice, tahini, sesame oil, Tabasco, and olive oil and crush the chickpeas using a potato masher or large fork. Season with salt and pepper. Serve at room temperature.

Simple taverna food at its best, this dish is incredibly good for you. Sardines, beloved by the Greeks and underused here in America, are chock-full of heart-healthy omega-3s, as are walnuts. Add some anti-inflammatory garlic and you've got a meal that would make any cardiologist smile. Personally, I just love this dish because it tastes amazing. **SERVES 4**

GRILLED SARDINES
WITH *garlic-walnut sauce*

SARDINES
2 pounds sardines (about 15), gutted
Grated zest and juice of 1 lemon
Kosher salt and freshly ground black
  pepper
¼ cup canola oil
¼ cup fresh flat-leaf parsley leaves

GARLIC-WALNUT SAUCE
½ cup extra-virgin olive oil
3 garlic cloves
1 cup whole walnuts, lightly toasted
Grated zest and juice of 1 lemon
1 cup chopped fresh flat-leaf parsley
  leaves
Kosher salt and freshly ground black
  pepper

1 Prepare the sardines: Put the sardines in a bowl, add the lemon juice and 2 teaspoons salt, cover, and refrigerate for 1 hour.

2 Make the sauce: Heat the olive oil in a large sauté pan over medium heat, add the garlic, and cook until lightly golden brown, about 2 minutes.

3 Put the walnuts in a food processor along with the garlic oil (including the cloves), lemon zest, and lemon juice, and pulse until combined. If the mixture is too thick, add a little water; the mixture should be a pourable vinaigrette with some texture. Add the parsley, season with salt and pepper, and pulse a few times to incorporate.

4 Heat your grill to high for direct grilling (see page 23).

5 Remove the sardines from the bowl and pat dry with paper towels. Brush them with the canola oil and season with pepper. Grill the sardines until golden brown and slightly charred, about 3 minutes. Flip them over and continue grilling for another minute.

6 Remove the sardines to a platter, drizzle with the garlic-walnut sauce, and garnish with the parsley leaves and lemon zest.

Vera Cruz salsa—tomato based and studded with garlic, chiles, olives, and capers—
is indigenous to Mexico's Gulf Coast and most often served with huachinango,
or red snapper. Some recipes are traditional for a reason—they've withstood the
test of time—and don't merit much in the way of tweaking. I do put a small but
impactful spin on the dish by grilling the salsa's tomatoes, bell peppers, and chiles for
an extra dimension of flavor and by leaving the sauce more chunky than smooth. If
you can't find one large fish, use two or four smaller ones, adjusting the cooking time
accordingly. **SERVES 4**

1 tablespoon coriander seeds
2 tablespoons achiote seeds
1 tablespoon dried Mexican oregano
1 tablespoon mild Spanish paprika
Kosher salt and freshly ground black
   pepper
Juice of 2 limes
2 garlic cloves, chopped
¼ cup canola oil
1 (4-pound) red snapper or black bass,
   scaled and gutted
Grilled Vera Cruz Salsa (recipe follows)
Fresh cilantro leaves, for garnish
Fresh thyme sprigs, for garnish

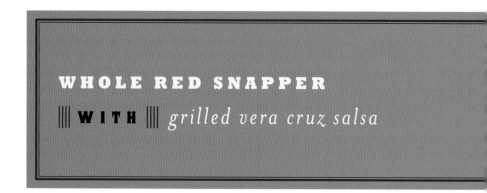

WHOLE RED SNAPPER
WITH *grilled vera cruz salsa*

1 Heat your grill to high for indirect grilling (see page 23).

2 Combine the coriander, achiote, and oregano in a small sauté pan and toast over low heat until just fragrant, about 2 minutes. Let cool slightly and then grind in a clean coffee grinder.

3 Combine the ground spices with the paprika, 1½ teaspoons salt, and ½ teaspoon pepper in a large baking dish. Add the lime juice, garlic, and oil and whisk to make a smooth paste. Rub the paste over the snapper and inside the cavity. Cover and marinate at room temperature for 20 minutes.

4 Remove the snapper from the marinade, make 3 slashes across the top, and season with salt and pepper. Grill, top side down, directly over the heat until slightly charred and golden brown, about 5 minutes. Carefully flip over the fish using a large heavy-duty spatula and move to the cooler side of the grill (indirect heat). Close the cover and continue cooking until the fish is just cooked through, about 30 minutes.

5 Spoon the salsa onto a large platter, put the snapper on top, and garnish with cilantro and thyme.

GRILLED VERA CRUZ SALSA

SERVES 4

8 plum tomatoes
2 red bell peppers
2 serrano chiles
4 tablespoons canola oil
Kosher salt and freshly ground black
    pepper
1 dried pasilla chile
2 garlic cloves, thinly sliced
1 cup pitted Manzanilla olives, chopped
1 tablespoon brined capers, drained
2 teaspoons fresh thyme, finely chopped
1 teaspoon dried Mexican oregano, lightly
    toasted
¼ cup chopped fresh cilantro leaves
3 tablespoons aged sherry vinegar
¼ cup extra-virgin olive oil

1. Heat your grill to high for direct grilling (see page 23).

2. Brush the tomatoes, bell peppers, and serranos with 3 tablespoons of the canola oil and season with salt and pepper. Grill until charred on all sides and just cooked through, about 8 minutes. Remove the tomatoes to a cutting board and let cool slightly. Roughly chop the tomatoes. Remove the bell peppers and serranos to a bowl, cover with plastic wrap, and let steam for 10 minutes. Peel, seed, and roughly chop.

3. Meanwhile, soak the pasilla chile in hot water for 30 minutes. Drain, seed, and then finely dice.

4. Heat 1 tablespoon of the canola oil in a small sauté pan over medium-low heat, add the garlic, and cook until soft, about 1 minute. Remove from the heat.

5. Combine the tomatoes, bell peppers, serrano and pasilla chiles, garlic, olives, capers, thyme, oregano, cilantro, vinegar, and olive oil in a medium bowl and season with salt and pepper. Let sit at room temperature for 30 minutes before serving to allow the flavors to meld.

Dorade, also known as sea bream, is a delicate, white-fleshed fish from the Mediterranean, with a succulent, meaty flavor. Add a dressing (stuffing to you northerners) of sweet crabmeat and you end up with a dish of some of the very best flavors the sea has to offer. The creamy vinaigrette is made with a light touch; its fresh lemony taste enhances the seafood without overpowering their delicate nature. I serve this dish at my restaurant Bar Americain, where it is a customer favorite as well as one of mine. Often I will drizzle it with parsley oil, a blend of 2 parts canola oil to 1 part parsley leaves, pureed until smooth, strained, and seasoned with salt. **SERVES 4**

¾ pound jumbo lump crabmeat, picked over

¼ cup chopped fresh flat-leaf parsley leaves

¼ cup thinly sliced green onion, green and pale green parts

2 tablespoons finely chopped fresh tarragon

Creamy Lemon Vinaigrette (recipe follows)

2 tablespoons extra-virgin olive oil

Kosher salt and freshly ground black pepper

½ pound (2 sticks) unsalted butter, at room temperature

4 tablespoons fresh dill, chopped, plus more for serving

4 (1- to 1½-pound) whole dorades, scaled, gutted, and skin scored

Canola oil

2 tablespoons Old Bay seasoning

2 lemons, halved

Celery leaves

WHOLE DORADE
||| **WITH** ||| *crabmeat dressing* ||| **AND** |||
creamy lemon vinaigrette

1 Combine the crabmeat, parsley, green onion, and tarragon in a medium bowl. Fold in ¼ cup of the vinaigrette and the olive oil and season with salt and pepper. Cover and refrigerate for at least 30 minutes to let the flavors meld. Remove the crabmeat dressing from the refrigerator 30 minutes before serving.

2 Stir together the butter and 3 table-spoons of the dill and season with salt and pepper. Cover and refrigerate while you prepare the dorade. (The butter can be made 1 day in advance and stored, covered, in the refrigerator. Remove from the refrigerator 10 minutes before using.)

3 Heat your grill to high for indirect grilling (see page 23). Put 2 large seasoned cast-iron pans on the grill over the heat source and let heat until smoking.

4 Brush the fish inside and out with canola oil and season with salt and pepper and the Old Bay. Place 2 fish in each of the hot pans and cook until the bottom side is golden brown, about 4 minutes. Flip over the fish and cook until lightly golden brown, about 3 minutes. Divide the butter between the pans, let it melt, and use it to baste the fish for about 2 minutes more.

5 Meanwhile, grill the lemons, cut sides down, until golden brown and caramelized, about 40 seconds.

6 Remove the fish to 4 plates, drizzle each with some of the lemon vinaigrette, and top with some of the crabmeat dressing. Garnish with the remaining 1 tablespoon fresh dill and the celery leaves. Serve the caramelized lemons on the side and squeeze over the fish just before eating.

CREAMY LEMON VINAIGRETTE
MAKES ABOUT 1 CUP

Grated zest of 1 lemon
3 tablespoons fresh lemon juice
1 tablespoon white wine vinegar
2 tablespoons mayonnaise
1 tablespoon Dijon mustard
1 teaspoon clover honey, or more to taste
Kosher salt and freshly ground black
    pepper
½ cup canola oil

Combine the lemon zest, lemon juice,
vinegar, mayonnaise, mustard, and honey
in a blender and blend until smooth.
Season with salt and pepper. With the
motor running, slowly add the oil and
blend until emulsified.

Meaty tuna steaks are a substantial platform for a golden mass of sweet onions scented with warm cinnamon. Fresh mint brings balance to the heady relish with its bright, fresh flavor and color. As is the case with so many dishes inspired by southern Italian cuisine, this one is a fun play of sweet-and-sour notes and is delicious served at room temperature. **SERVES 4**

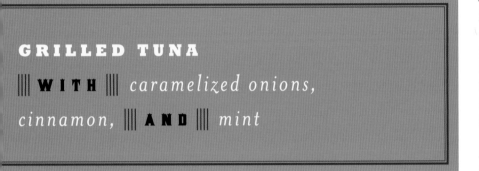

GRILLED TUNA
||| **WITH** ||| *caramelized onions, cinnamon,* ||| **AND** ||| *mint*

4 tablespoons canola oil
2 large Spanish onions, halved and thinly sliced
1 tablespoon sugar
Pinch of red pepper flakes
2 cinnamon sticks
¼ cup red wine vinegar
Kosher salt and freshly ground black pepper
4 (8-ounce) tuna steaks
2 tablespoons finely chopped fresh mint leaves

1 Heat 2 tablespoons of the oil in a large sauté pan over medium heat. Add the onions and sugar and cook until soft, about 10 minutes. Add the red pepper flakes and cinnamon and continue cooking, stirring occasionally, until lightly golden brown and caramelized, about 30 minutes longer. Stir in the vinegar and a few tablespoons water and season with salt and pepper.

2 Heat your grill to high for direct grilling (see page 23).

3 Brush the tuna on both sides with the remaining 2 tablespoons oil and season with salt and pepper. Grill until golden brown, slightly charred, and cooked to medium-rare, about 2 minutes per side.

4 Remove the tuna to a platter. Discard the cinnamon sticks from the onion relish and stir in the mint. Top the tuna with the relish. Let sit at room temperature for about 15 minutes before serving.

Red slaw, also known as Lexington slaw for the North Carolina town it comes from, is coleslaw with just a touch of barbecue flavor added to it. The Carolina classic is made without mayonnaise, and while you can certainly leave it out of this recipe, I like the creamy texture that just a few tablespoons add. The slaw is the perfect way to round out sandwiches starring sweet, slightly briny soft-shell crabs, but would also be phenomenal atop pulled pork or grilled chicken. **SERVES 4**

GRILLED SOFT-SHELL CRAB SANDWICHES ||| WITH ||| *red slaw* ||| AND ||| *yellow tomatoes*

¼ cup ketchup
2 tablespoons mayonnaise
2 tablespoons sugar
2 tablespoons apple cider vinegar
1 teaspoon celery salt
⅛ teaspoon cayenne
Kosher salt and freshly ground black pepper
½ small head white cabbage, cored and finely shredded
4 large soft-shell crabs, cleaned
¼ cup canola oil
8 tablespoons (1 stick) unsalted butter, softened
4 soft hamburger buns, split
1 yellow tomato, cut into ¼-inch-thick slices
Chopped green onion, for garnish

1 Whisk together the ketchup, mayonnaise, sugar, vinegar, celery salt, cayenne, 1 teaspoon kosher salt, and ¼ teaspoon black pepper in a large bowl. Add the cabbage and toss to combine. Cover and refrigerate for at least 1 hour and up to 24 hours before serving. Taste for seasoning just before serving.

2 Heat your grill to high for direct grilling (see page 23).

3 Brush both sides of the crabs with the oil and season with salt and pepper. Grill until the crabs are just firm to the touch, about 4 minutes per side.

4 Spread the butter onto the split sides of the buns and grill, buttered side down, until lightly browned, about 20 seconds.

5 Spoon some slaw onto the bottom of each bun and top with tomato and a crab. Garnish with green onion.

Sweet, delicate Dungeness crabs live in the waters of the Pacific Northwest. This dish pays homage to the fact that the region is also home to a prominent Asian American community. I steam the crabs on the grill with soy sauce and ginger—using the grates of the grill like a stovetop. Golden mirin, a rice cooking wine, balances the saltiness of soy; warm sesame oil adds a touch of richness; and tart lime keeps this light dish fresh.

SERVES 4

2 tablespoons canola oil
4 shallots, finely diced
½ cup sliced fresh ginger
1 cup fish stock or vegetable stock
1 cup low-sodium soy sauce
1 cup mirin
3 limes, halved
4 large (2- to 3-pound) Dungeness crabs, cleaned
2 tablespoons clover honey
¼ teaspoon coarsely ground black pepper
2 teaspoons toasted sesame oil
Pinch of red pepper flakes
2 tablespoons chopped fresh cilantro leaves

DUNGENESS CRAB STEAMED ON THE GRILL IN GINGER, SOY, AND LIME

1 Heat your grill to high for direct grilling (see page 23).

2 Heat the canola oil in a medium roasting pan on the grates of the grill. Add the shallots and ginger and cook for 1 minute. Add the fish stock, soy sauce, and mirin. Squeeze the juice from the limes into the pan and add the lime halves, too. Bring to a boil. Add the crabs, close the cover on the grill, and steam until the crabs are just cooked through, about 12 minutes. Remove the crabs to a platter.

3 Pour the steaming liquid into a bowl, whisk in the honey, black pepper, sesame oil, red pepper flakes, and cilantro and let cool slightly. Serve on the side with the crabs.

Crawfish are an inherent part of Louisiana culture; crawfish boils are a time-honored way to bring friends and family together. Eating crawfish (you eat only the tails) is a messy endeavor—this is fun food. I like the roasted, intense flavor that grilling the crawfish brings out, and this butter is a perfect match for shellfish. Mixed with anise-flavored tarragon and peppery, vinegary Tabasco, it's seriously lip-smacking stuff. Feel free to use another brand of hot sauce if you prefer.

When purchasing crawfish, buy live ones that are active and heavy for their size. "Select" or "#1 Select" are words regularly used to describe larger crawfish, those that range from twelve to fifteen per pound. Some sorting methods during the late-spring and early-summer months will classify an even larger grade as "True Select," with twelve or fewer crawfish per pound. Either of these is perfect for this recipe, which keeps things simple. **SERVES 6**

CRAWFISH COOKED IN A GRILL BASKET ||| WITH |||

tabasco-tarragon butter

¾ pound (3 sticks) unsalted butter, slightly softened
¼ cup chopped fresh tarragon
¼ cup Tabasco sauce
¼ teaspoon cayenne
Kosher salt and freshly ground black pepper
5 pounds Select or True Select live crawfish

1 Combine the butter, tarragon, Tabasco, and cayenne in a food processor and process until smooth; season with salt and pepper. Scrape into a bowl, cover, and refrigerate for at least 1 hour to allow the flavors to meld. Remove from the refrigerator 1 hour before using.

2 Bring a large stockpot of salted water to a boil. Have ready a large bowl filled halfway with ice water. Working in batches, add the crawfish, head first, to the boiling water and cook for 30 seconds. Remove to the ice bath to cool and then drain well.

3 Lay the crawfish, belly side up, on a cutting board. Using a sharp knife, cut through the shell of each body, beginning at the head and finishing at the tail; this allows the heat to penetrate through the shell to grill the meat evenly. Remove the intestine, a thin vein running the length of the body of the crawfish. Remove the sack located behind the eyes. Crack the shell on the legs of the crawfish to allow heat to penetrate. Rinse thoroughly with cold water.

4 Heat your grill to medium-high for direct grilling (see page 23).

5 Put half of the tarragon butter in a small saucepan and heat over low heat until melted. Put the crawfish, cut side up, in a large grill basket (work in batches, if need be), brush the meat with some of the butter, and season with salt and pepper. Grill, cut side up, until the shells turn bright red, 2 to 5 minutes. Flip over the crawfish to grill the other side, brushing with more of the melted butter, 2 to 5 minutes.

6 Remove the crawfish to a platter and top with the remaining butter.

There might not be a more New England dish than the lobster roll. While I love that super-traditional dish as much as the next person, I do have room in my heart for other lobster sandwiches. This one heads south and west from the Down East locale in which it originated. Sweet corn echoes the lobster's sweet flavor and creamy avocado doubles up the richness. **SERVES 6**

4 (2-pound) live lobsters
8 ears of corn
Kosher salt and freshly ground black
    pepper
Canola oil
1 serrano chile
3 ripe Hass avocados, peeled, pitted, and
    diced
¼ cup crème fraîche
½ small red onion, finely diced
¼ cup chopped fresh cilantro leaves
Juice of 2 limes
Few dashes of Tabasco sauce
6 soft sesame seed buns, split
Fresh flat-leaf parsley, for garnish

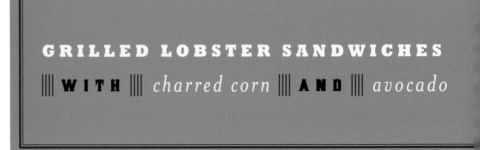

GRILLED LOBSTER SANDWICHES
||| **WITH** ||| *charred corn* ||| **AND** ||| *avocado*

1 Bring a large pot of salted water to a boil. Working in batches, add the lobsters and boil for 10 to 12 minutes; they will be about three-quarters done. Drain well and let cool. The lobsters can be parboiled a few hours in advance, covered, and kept refrigerated. Bring to room temperature before grilling.
2 Heat your grill to high for direct grilling (see page 23).
3 Pull the outer husks down each ear of corn to the base. Strip away the silk from each ear of corn. Fold the husks back into place and tie the ends together with kitchen string. Place the ears of corn in a large bowl of cold water with 1 tablespoon salt for 10 minutes.
4 Remove the corn from the water and shake off the excess. Put the corn on the grill, close the cover, and grill, turning every

5 minutes, for 15 minutes, or until the kernels are almost tender when pierced with a paring knife.
5 Peel back the husks and remove. Brush the corn with oil and season with salt and pepper. Grill the ears until the kernels are lightly golden brown on all sides, about 5 minutes. Use a sharp knife to remove the kernels from the ears.
6 Brush the serrano with oil and grill, turning as needed, until charred all over, 6 to 8 minutes. Remove to a bowl, cover, and let sit for 10 minutes. Peel, seed, and roughly chop.
7 Put the avocados and crème fraîche in a medium bowl and mash slightly with a fork. Add the corn kernels, chile, diced red onion, cilantro, lime juice, Tabasco, and

2 tablespoons of oil. Season with salt and pepper and gently stir to combine.
8 Split each lobster down the underside with a heavy knife, taking care not to cut through the back shell, so that the lobster is still in one piece but the inside flesh is halved and exposed. Brush the cut sides of the lobsters with oil and season with salt and pepper. Grill the lobsters, cut side down, until lightly charred and heated through, 5 to 7 minutes.
9 Toast the buns, split side down, on the grill until lightly golden brown, about 20 seconds.
10 Remove the lobster meat from the shells and coarsely chop. Fill each bun with lobster, charred corn and avocado, and some parsley leaves.

Grilled lobster tails are quick and easy, and, best of all, lobster always impresses. Grilling intensifies the already succulent meat's sweet flavor. A simple compound butter, fresh with lemon juice and bright zest and flecked with the red fruity heat of Fresno chiles, finishes the dish with sophisticated, luscious flavor. I serve a spin on this dish as a weekly special at Mesa Grill, and it is a customer favorite. **SERVES 8**

GRILLED LOBSTER TAILS
||| **WITH** ||| *lemon-fresno butter*

1 cup fresh lemon juice
½ teaspoon clover honey
½ pound (2 sticks) unsalted butter, softened
2 teaspoons grated lemon zest
2 red Fresno chiles, grilled, seeded, and finely diced (see page 122)
Kosher salt and freshly ground black pepper
8 jumbo (14- to 16-ounce) Maine lobster tails
Canola oil
Chopped fresh chives, for garnish

1 Put the lemon juice in a small saucepan and bring to a boil over high heat. Cook until reduced to ¼ cup. Stir in the honey and let cool.

2 Mix together the butter, the reduced lemon juice, and the lemon zest until smooth. Fold in the Fresno chiles and season with salt and pepper. Cover and refrigerate for at least 1 hour or up to 1 week to allow the flavors to meld.

3 Heat your grill to high for direct grilling (see page 23).

4 Bring a large pot of salted water to a boil. Add the lobster tails and boil until parboiled, 6 minutes. Drain well. Split each lobster tail lengthwise down the underside with a heavy knife, taking care not to cut through the back shell so that the lobster is still in one piece but the flesh is halved and exposed.

5 Brush the flesh side of each lobster tail with oil and season with salt and pepper. Grill, flesh side down, until slightly charred, 2 to 3 minutes. Flip over the lobster tails and continue grilling until just cooked through, 2 to 3 minutes.

6 Serve immediately, garnished with chives.

Mojo, the addictively delicious Cuban marinade of garlic, tart citrus, and olive oil, gets an update with the addition of a peppery poblano chile and charred jalapeño. Bright cilantro turns the sauce as green as it tastes. The assertive flavors are a perfect match for the sweet, mild taste of langoustine tails. If you can't find langoustines, you could try this with their larger cousin the Atlantic lobster or with large prawns for a similar end result. **SERVES 4 TO 6**

1 large poblano chile (or 2 small)
1 jalapeño
Canola oil
¼ cup fresh lime juice
3 garlic cloves, chopped
¼ teaspoon ground coriander
¼ cup packed fresh cilantro or flat-leaf
    parsley leaves, plus more for garnish
⅓ cup extra-virgin olive oil
1 teaspoon clover honey
Kosher salt and freshly ground black
    pepper
12 langoustines, shells on
Hot sauce

GRILLED LANGOUSTINES
||| **WITH** ||| *green chile mojo*

1 Heat your grill to high for direct grilling (see page 23).
2 Brush the poblano and jalapeño with canola oil and grill, turning as needed, until charred all over, about 8 minutes. Remove to a bowl, cover, and let sit for 10 minutes. Peel, seed, and roughly chop.
3 Combine the chopped chiles, lime juice, ¼ cup water, the garlic, coriander, cilantro, olive oil, and honey and mix until smooth. Season with salt and pepper. If the mojo is too thick, add a few tablespoons of water to loosen.

4 Brush the undersides of the langoustines with canola oil and season with salt and pepper. Grill for 2 minutes, then turn over the langoustines, and grill for another minute.
5 Put the langoustines on a platter, garnish with cilantro, and drizzle with hot sauce. Serve the mojo on the side.

Clams Casino was born nearly one hundred years ago at the Little Casino in Narragansett, Rhode Island. Created by maître d'hôtel Julius Keller to fulfill the request for "something special" for a wealthy patron in 1917, the dish was soon embraced by the Italian American community and has since become an American classic. There have been variations on the dish since then, with some folks saying there has to be pimiento or other cheese, but one thing always remains the same: You must start with deliciously briny clams and seal the deal with bacon. When well done, these are salty, smoky things of beauty. **SERVES 4 TO 6**

3 tablespoons panko bread crumbs

4 ounces (8 strips) double-smoked bacon, finely diced

2 shallots, finely diced

1 small Fresno chile, finely diced

1 teaspoon grated lemon zest

3 tablespoons finely chopped fresh flat-leaf parsley leaves, plus whole leaves for garnish

Kosher salt and freshly ground black pepper

Extra-virgin olive oil

36 littleneck or cherrystone clams, soaked in water and scrubbed

Lemon wedges

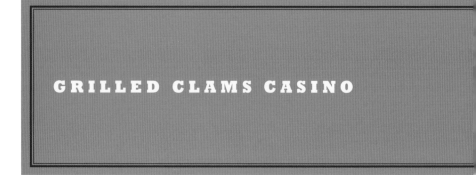

GRILLED CLAMS CASINO

1 Heat your grill to high for direct grilling (see page 23).

2 Heat a sauté pan over low heat, add the bread crumbs, and toast, stirring constantly, until lightly golden brown, about 5 minutes. Remove to a small bowl.

3 Return the pan to the stove over medium heat and cook the bacon until golden brown and crisp, and the fat has rendered, about 10 minutes. Remove the bacon with a slotted spoon to a plate lined with paper towels.

4 Add the shallots and Fresno chile to the fat in the pan and cook until soft, about

2 minutes. Return the bacon and bread crumbs to the pan and toss to coat. Add the lemon zest and chopped parsley and season with salt and pepper; if needed, add olive oil to moisten slightly. Remove from the heat.

5 Put the clams directly on the grates of the grill, close the cover, and cook until all the clams have opened, 3 to 4 minutes (discard any that do not).

6 Remove the clams to a platter and top each with some of the bacon mixture. Drizzle with more olive oil, garnish with parsley leaves, and serve with lemon wedges on the side.

Greece is one of my favorite travel destinations and a big reason for that is its cuisine. The food is just so fresh and delicious, and this grilled seafood salad is a great example. Cold-smoked tomatoes, flavored with smoke but not cooked, add tons of flavor to the cool and salty relish. The squid cooks very quickly, so beware of overcooking. **SERVES 4**

GRILLED SHRIMP ||| AND ||| CALAMARI ||| WITH ||| *smoked tomato—black olive relish*

SMOKED TOMATO—BLACK OLIVE RELISH

8 plum tomatoes, cored

Canola oil

Kosher salt and freshly ground black pepper

½ cup extra-virgin olive oil, plus more for drizzling

½ cup pitted kalamata olives, coarsely chopped

½ small red onion, finely diced

¼ cup chopped fresh dill

¼ cup chopped fresh flat-leaf parsley leaves

¼ cup fresh lemon juice

1 tablespoon red wine vinegar

1 teaspoon clover honey

GRILLED SEAFOOD

12 small squid, cleaned

12 colossal (U-15 or U-10) shrimp, tails on, shelled and deveined

¼ cup canola oil, plus more for brushing

¼ cup fresh lemon juice, plus 4 lemons, halved

4 garlic cloves, minced

Kosher salt and freshly ground black pepper

Fresh dill sprigs, for garnish

recipe continues >>

1 Soak 1 cup of apple wood chips for at least 30 minutes.

2 Heat your grill to very low for indirect grilling (see page 23).

3 If using a charcoal grill, scatter the drained wood chips over the coals. If the temperature in the grill is hotter than 100°F, put 2 cups of ice cubes in an aluminum tray and nestle the tray next to the coals on the bottom grate. Put the cooking grate in place. If using a gas grill, put the drained wood chips in a smoker box. Add a tray of ice cubes, if needed, to the cooking grate. Then, for either grill, close the cover and let smoke build until the temperature in the grill reaches 100°F.

4 Make the relish: Brush the tomatoes with canola oil, season with salt and pepper, and arrange in a single layer on the grill.

Cover the grill and cold-smoke the tomatoes for 10 to 20 minutes, depending on how smoky you want them.

5 Coarsely chop the tomatoes, transfer to a bowl, and add the olive oil, olives, red onion, dill, parsley, lemon juice, vinegar, and honey; season with salt and pepper. Let the relish sit at room temperature until ready to use.

6 Heat your grill to high for direct grilling (see page 23). If using wood skewers, soak them in water for at least 15 minutes.

7 Prepare the seafood: Separate the heads and tentacles from the squid. Slit the bodies through one side to butterfly them so that they lie flat. Put the squid (bodies, heads, and tentacles) and shrimp in 2 separate bowls. Divide the canola oil, lemon juice, and garlic between the

bowls, and season with salt and pepper. Toss to combine and then let marinate for 15 minutes.

8 Thread the shrimp and squid tentacles and heads on separate skewers and season with salt and pepper. Grill the shrimp for about 2 minutes per side and the squid tentacles and heads for about 30 seconds per side. Put the squid bodies directly on the grill and cook for about 15 seconds per side.

9 Brush the cut side of each lemon half with canola oil and season with salt and pepper. Grill the lemons, cut side down, until slightly charred. Remove to a plate.

10 Arrange the skewers and squid bodies on a large platter. Top with the relish, drizzle with olive oil, and squeeze 1 grilled lemon half over everything. Garnish with dill sprigs and the remaining grilled lemon halves.

Garam masala, used in the marinade along with red chile powder for just a touch of heat, is a slightly sweet, aromatic Indian spice mixture usually containing coriander, cumin, cinnamon, and lots of black pepper. There's a good amount of sunny lemon juice in the marinade for this fresh dish, but because of that lemon juice, you have to keep the marinating time to just fifteen minutes lest the acid begin to "cook" the delicate shrimp. A Thai chile adds an authentic burst of heat to the herbaceous chutney, but if you can't find one, you could substitute a serrano chile for less heat— or a habanero for more. **SERVES 4**

SHRIMP
Juice of 2 lemons
1 teaspoon garam masala
1 teaspoon red chile powder, such as ancho or New Mexican
¼ cup canola oil
1 pound large (21 to 24 count) shrimp, tails left on, shelled and deveined

CILANTRO-MINT CHUTNEY
1 cup tightly packed fresh cilantro leaves, plus more for garnish
½ cup tightly packed fresh mint leaves
4 green onions, white and green parts, chopped
1 Thai chile, finely minced
Grated zest of 1 lime
1 to 2 tablespoons clover honey, to taste
3 tablespoons canola oil
Kosher salt and freshly ground black pepper

GRILLED SHRIMP SKEWERS
||| **WITH** ||| *cilantro-mint chutney*

1 Heat your grill to high for direct grilling (see page 23). If using wood skewers, soak them in cold water for at least 15 minutes.

2 Marinate the shrimp: Whisk together the lemon juice, garam masala, chile powder, and oil in a medium bowl. Add the shrimp and toss to coat in the mixture. Let sit to marinate for 15 minutes.

3 Make the chutney: Combine the cilantro, mint, green onions, Thai chile, and lime zest in a food processor and pulse until coarsely chopped. Add 1 tablespoon of the honey and the oil and pulse until a slightly loose mixture, adding a little water if needed; season with salt and pepper and the remaining 1 tablespoon honey if needed.

4 Thread 3 shrimp onto each skewer so that the shrimp lie flat. Season with salt and pepper and grill until golden brown, slightly charred on both sides, and just cooked through, about 1½ minutes per side.

5 Remove the shrimp to a platter, serve with the chutney, and garnish with cilantro leaves.

"Barbecue" means many things to many people, and in New Orleans "barbecue shrimp" means shrimp sautéed in a garlicky butter sauce with a heavy dose of Worcestershire. I know it looks like a lot of butter for the amount of shrimp, but butter is key in creating the right consistency and flavor in this indulgent sauce. Believe me, you'll be fighting over who gets to take the last swipe at the pan with that French bread. You'll want to mop up every last bit of that buttery goodness.

SERVES 4

½ pound (2 sticks) unsalted butter
4 garlic cloves, chopped
2 teaspoons smoked mild paprika
2 tablespoons Worcestershire sauce
Few dashes of Tabasco sauce
1 lemon, halved
1 tablespoon chopped fresh rosemary
½ teaspoon freshly ground black pepper,
    plus more to taste
Kosher salt
1 pound large (21 to 24 count) shrimp,
    peeled and deveined
Canola oil
2 tablespoons chopped fresh flat-leaf
    parsley leaves
French bread, sliced ¼-inch thick

GRILLED NEW ORLEANS "BBQ" SHRIMP

1 Heat your grill to high for direct grilling (see page 23).

2 Melt the butter in a large sauté pan over medium heat. Add the garlic and cook for 30 seconds. Add the paprika and cook for 10 seconds. Add the Worcestershire, Tabasco, juice of ½ lemon, the rosemary, and ½ teaspoon pepper. Season with salt and keep warm.

3 Thinly slice the remaining lemon half.

4 Toss the shrimp in canola oil and season with salt and pepper. Grill until lightly charred and just cooked through, about 1½ minutes per side. Remove from the grill and immediately toss in the butter sauce in the pan. Add the parsley and lemon slices and cook for 10 seconds. Transfer to shallow bowls.

5 Grill the bread until it has grill marks on both sides, about 30 seconds per side. Serve the shrimp and sauce with the grilled bread for dipping.

One of the most common tapas of Spain, gambas al ajillo, *is quick, easy, and full of garlic flavor. Grilled tomato bread is another popular tapa and is often served alongside the shrimp; you have to have something tasty to use to sop up all of that garlic-scented oil of the shrimp. Serving the two directly together in this way just saves you a step.* **SERVES 4 TO 6**

GARLIC SHRIMP SERVED ON GRILLED TOMATO BREAD

GARLIC SHRIMP
½ cup plus 2 tablespoons extra-virgin
   olive oil, plus more for drizzling
12 garlic cloves, chopped
¼ teaspoon red pepper flakes
¼ cup dry sherry
2 teaspoons chopped fresh thyme
Kosher salt and freshly ground black
   pepper
1 pound medium (36 to 40 count) shrimp,
   shelled and deveined
¼ cup chopped fresh flat-leaf parsley
   leaves

GRILLED TOMATO BREAD
6 plum tomatoes
¼ cup canola oil
Kosher salt and freshly ground black
   pepper
¼ teaspoon smoked mild Spanish paprika
2 garlic cloves, finely chopped
Clover honey, if needed
French baguette, sliced ½ inch thick
Chopped fresh flat-leaf parsley leaves,
   for garnish

recipe continues >>

1 Prepare the shrimp: Heat 2 tablespoons of the olive oil in a small sauté pan over medium heat, add the garlic, and cook until soft, about 1 minute. Add the red pepper flakes and cook for 30 seconds. Add the sherry and thyme and cook until the liquid evaporates, about 2 minutes. Remove from the heat, transfer to a bowl, and whisk in the remaining ½ cup olive oil; season with salt and pepper.

2 Put the shrimp in a medium bowl, add ¼ cup of the garlic marinade, and toss to coat the shrimp. Cover and refrigerate for 30 minutes.

3 Meanwhile, heat your grill to high for direct grilling (see page 23).

4 Make the tomato bread: Brush the tomatoes with the canola oil and season with salt and pepper. Grill the tomatoes until charred on all sides and just soft, about 8 minutes.

5 Immediately transfer the tomatoes to a food processor, add the paprika and garlic, and pulse until coarsely chopped. Season with honey, if needed, and salt and pepper.

6 Grill the bread on both sides until lightly golden brown, about 30 seconds per side. Remove the bread to a platter and immediately spoon some of the tomato mixture on top of each slice. Garnish with chopped parsley.

7 Remove the shrimp from the marinade and season with salt and pepper. Grill until pink and just cooked through, about 1½ minutes per side.

8 Remove the shrimp from the grill to a clean bowl and toss with the remaining marinade and the parsley. Spoon shrimp over each slice of bread and drizzle with olive oil.

This is a great healthful dish that doesn't make you feel as though you're depriving yourself in the least. And you're not; there's way too much flavor from fresh sweet-hot ginger, pungent green onions, tart lime juice, creamy yogurt, and a smoky blend of chile powders. A relative of cabbage, Brussels sprouts, and broccoli, kale can be pungent and a bit tough when raw. Massaging it with the dressing helps break it down. The acid in the dressing "cooks" the kale, making it more supple with less of a bite. **SERVES 4**

KALE

Juice of 1 lime
1 tablespoon rice vinegar
1 teaspoon finely grated fresh ginger
2 teaspoons clover honey
Kosher salt and freshly ground
    black pepper
¼ cup canola oil
1 pound kale, stemmed and
    finely shredded

PRAWNS

4 tablespoons canola oil
2 garlic cloves, thinly sliced
1 small shallot, thinly sliced
1 (2-inch) piece fresh ginger,
    peeled and grated
2 tablespoons ancho chile powder
¼ teaspoon chile de árbol powder
1 cup whole milk Greek yogurt
2 tablespoons low-sodium soy sauce
Grated zest and juice of 1 lime
2 green onions, green and pale
    green parts, thinly sliced
Kosher salt and freshly ground
    black pepper
12 prawns, shelled and deveined
Chopped fresh chives, for garnish

1 Heat your grill to high for direct grilling (see page 23).

2 Marinate the kale: Whisk together the lime juice, rice vinegar, ginger, and honey in a large bowl; season with salt and pepper. Slowly whisk in the oil. Add the kale and massage the dressing into the leaves. Let sit at room temperature while you prepare the prawns.

3 Prepare the prawns: Heat 2 table-spoons of the oil in a small sauté pan over medium heat. Add the garlic, shallot, and ginger and cook until soft, about 2 minutes. Add the chile powders and cook for 30 seconds. Transfer to a large bowl and let cool for a few minutes. Stir in the yogurt, soy sauce, lime zest, lime juice, and green onions and season with salt and pepper.

4 Brush the prawns with the remaining 2 tablespoons oil and season with salt and pepper. Grill the prawns until golden brown and slightly charred on both sides, about 2 minutes per side. Remove the prawns from the grill and immediately toss in the yogurt mixture.

5 Transfer the kale to a platter, top with the prawns, and garnish with chives.

Most marinades are used to add flavor and tenderize protein before it is cooked; this dish reverses the process so that the acid, in this case fresh lemon juice, doesn't break down the delicate shellfish but still has the opportunity to infuse the dish with its bright flavor. The char in the shellfish is an important element of the dish—the blistery spots are an essential flavor component. This is best achieved by putting your dry pan on the grill and letting it heat before adding the oil-coated shellfish. The pan—cast iron is best—should be really hot. **SERVES 4 TO 6**

MARINATED CHARRED SEAFOOD SALAD

1 teaspoon grated lemon zest
2 tablespoons fresh lemon juice
2 tablespoons red wine vinegar
1 large garlic clove, smashed to a paste
Pinch of red pepper flakes
¼ cup extra-virgin olive oil
Kosher salt and freshly ground black
    pepper
1 pound large (21 to 24 count) shrimp,
    shelled and deveined
1 pound cleaned squid, tubes and
    tentacles
2 pounds mussels, bearded and scrubbed
4 tablespoons canola oil
½ red onion, halved lengthwise and thinly
    sliced
1 cup pitted Gaeta olives, halved
1 pint grape tomatoes, halved
½ cup loosely packed fresh flat-leaf
    parsley leaves
¼ cup chopped fresh basil leaves

1 Heat your grill to high for direct grilling (see page 23); alternatively you can use a grill pan.
2 Whisk together the lemon zest, lemon juice, vinegar, garlic, red pepper flakes, and olive oil in a bowl and season with salt and black pepper. Let sit at room temperature for at least 15 minutes to allow the flavors to meld.
3 Heat a cast-iron pan on the grill for 10 minutes.
4 Toss the shrimp, squid, and mussels separately with 2 tablespoons canola oil and season with salt and pepper. Add the shrimp to the pan and cook until golden brown on both sides and just cooked through, about 1 minute per side. Remove to a large bowl.

Add 2 tablespoons canola oil and the squid to the pan and cook until golden brown and just cooked through, about 1 minute per side; remove to the bowl with the shrimp. Add the mussels to the pan and cook, stirring occasionally, until the mussels open. Remove to a baking sheet and let cool slightly. Remove the meat from the shells and add to the shrimp and squid. (Discard any that do not open.)
5 Add the dressing to the seafood along with the onion, olives, and tomatoes and toss to combine. Season with salt and pepper and fold in the parsley and basil. Refrigerate for at least 1 hour and up to 8 hours before serving.

Deep red harissa is a fiery blend of dried chiles, garlic, caraway, coriander, and smoky cumin. This North African chile paste is an incredible way to create an instant surge of flavor; in this recipe, sweetly mild sea scallops get a boost from the paste. Rich and smooth tahini vinaigrette mellows the heat, and a fresh yet satisfying salad of cracked wheat loaded with parsley and dill rounds out this Middle Eastern— inspired dish. You can find many excellent prepared harissas and could certainly use one here, but making your own allows you to control the intensity. **SERVES 4**

HARISSA SCALLOPS

3 dried ancho chiles, lightly toasted
1 New Mexican red chile, lightly toasted
2 chiles de árbol, lightly toasted
3 tablespoons extra-virgin olive oil
3 garlic cloves, minced
Kosher salt and freshly ground black
    pepper
1 teaspoon ground coriander
1 teaspoon ground caraway
½ teaspoon ground cumin
1 tablespoon canola oil
12 large sea scallops, patted dry
Tahini Vinaigrette (recipe follows)

CRACKED WHEAT SALAD

Kosher salt and freshly ground black
    pepper
1 cup cracked wheat
¼ cup chopped fresh flat-leaf parsley
    leaves
¼ cup chopped fresh dill
2 tablespoons finely chopped fresh mint
    leaves
½ English cucumber, cut into small dice
½ pint grape tomatoes, halved
Juice of 1 lemon
¼ cup extra-virgin olive oil

HARISSA SEA SCALLOPS

||| **WITH** ||| *cracked wheat salad* ||| **AND** ||| *tahini vinaigrette*

1 Start the harissa: Soak the three kinds of dried chiles in hot water for 30 minutes. Drain, reserving the soaking liquid.

2 Remove the stems and seeds from the chiles and transfer the chiles to a food processor. Add the olive oil, garlic, 1 teaspoon salt, coriander, caraway, cumin, and a few tablespoons of the soaking liquid. Process the mixture to a smooth paste, adding more soaking liquid if needed. Scrape into a bowl.

3 Heat your grill to high for direct grilling (see page 23).

4 Make the cracked wheat salad: Bring 2 cups salted water to a boil, add the cracked wheat, cover, and simmer over medium heat until the wheat is tender and the water is absorbed, about 30 minutes. Remove from the heat and let sit, covered, for 5 minutes.

5 Fluff the cracked wheat with a fork and transfer to a bowl. Add the parsley, dill, mint, cucumber, tomatoes, lemon juice, and olive oil and season with salt and pepper.

6 Whisk together 2 tablespoons of the harissa and the canola oil in a shallow bowl. Season the scallops on both sides with salt and pepper and dredge in the harissa mixture. Grill on both sides until slightly charred and just cooked through, about 1½ minutes per side.

7 Serve the scallops over the cracked wheat salad, drizzle with tahini vinaigrette, and serve extra harissa on the side.

TAHINI VINAIGRETTE

MAKES ABOUT 1 CUP

Pinch of saffron
3 tablespoons aged sherry vinegar
1 grilled or jarred roasted red bell pepper,
    peeled, seeded, and chopped
2 garlic cloves, chopped
¼ cup tahini
1 tablespoon clover honey
Kosher salt and freshly ground black
    pepper
½ cup canola oil

Steep the saffron in ¼ cup hot water for
5 minutes to bloom. Transfer the saffron
mixture to a blender and add the vinegar,
roasted pepper, garlic, tahini, and honey
and blend until smooth. Season with salt
and pepper. With the motor running,
slowly drizzle in the oil and blend until
emulsified. (The vinaigrette can be
made up to 4 hours in advance, covered,
and kept refrigerated. Bring to room
temperature before serving.)

Plump sea scallops are always crowd-pleasers. Skewering the scallops makes them a breeze to serve and move on and off of the grill. Meaty though they may be, scallops are still somewhat fragile; the oil keeps them from sticking or tearing. **SERVES 4**

GRILLED SEA SCALLOP SKEWERS ‖ WITH ‖ *creamy hot*
pepper-garlic vinaigrette

½ cup mayonnaise
¼ cup jarred hot cherry peppers, chopped, plus slices for garnish
2 teaspoons finely chopped fresh thyme
2 tablespoons red wine vinegar
2 tablespoons fresh lemon juice
2 tablespoons Dijon mustard
2 garlic cloves, finely chopped
Kosher salt and freshly ground black pepper
Canola oil
4 slices good white bread, crusts removed, finely processed (1 cup fresh bread crumbs)
1 tablespoon finely chopped fresh flat-leaf parsley leaves, plus more for garnish
1 teaspoon grated lemon zest
20 sea scallops, patted dry

1 Whisk together the mayonnaise, cherry peppers, thyme, vinegar, lemon juice, mustard, and garlic in a bowl and season with salt and pepper. Cover and refrigerate for at least 30 minutes to allow the flavors to meld.

2 Heat your grill to high for direct grilling (see page 23). If using wood skewers, soak them in cold water for at least 15 minutes.

3 Heat a few tablespoons oil in a medium sauté pan over medium heat. Add the bread crumbs and cook until lightly golden brown, about 5 minutes. Remove from the heat, stir in the parsley and lemon zest, and season with salt and pepper.

4 Thread each scallop onto 2 skewers so that the scallops lie flat. Brush on both sides with oil and season with salt and pepper. Grill until lightly golden brown on both sides and just cooked through, about 1½ minutes per side.

5 Drizzle some of the mayonnaise vinaigrette on a platter and top with the scallops. Sprinkle the bread crumbs over the scallops and garnish with hot cherry pepper slices and chopped parsley. Serve the remaining vinaigrette on the side.

Crisp cubes of salty pancetta add a salty depth of flavor to plump and briny oysters. I lace a peppercorn-packed vinegary mignonette, oysters' traditional accompaniment, with vibrant basil and sweet tomato to up the Italian influence and add freshness.

SERVES 4

1 tablespoon canola oil
4 ounces pancetta, finely diced
2 tablespoons finely diced shallot
1 large plum tomato, seeded and finely diced
6 fresh basil leaves, finely chopped
¼ cup aged balsamic or red wine vinegar
¼ teaspoon coarsely ground black peppercorns
Kosher salt
20 oysters, soaked in water and scrubbed well
Fresh flat-leaf parsley leaves, for garnish
Extra-virgin olive oil

GRILLED OYSTERS ||| WITH |||
crispy pancetta–tomato–basil mignonette

1 Soak 1 cup almond or apple wood chips in water for at least 30 minutes.

2 Heat your grill to high for direct grilling (see page 23).

3 Meanwhile, heat the canola oil in a small sauté pan over medium heat. Add the pancetta and cook until crisp and the fat has rendered, about 8 minutes. Add the shallot and cook for 1 minute. Remove from the heat and add the tomato, basil, vinegar, and pepper. Season with salt and keep warm.

4 Add the drained wood chips to the coals in a charcoal grill or put them in a smoker box of a gas grill. Close the cover and let smoke build for 10 minutes.

5 Evenly spread 1 cup salt on a large platter.

6 Grip each oyster, flat side up, in a folded kitchen towel and work over a bowl. Find the small opening between the shells near the hinge and pry it open with an oyster knife, catching the delicious juices, known as the oyster liquor, in the bottom shell and the overflow in the bowl. Cut the oyster meat loose from the top shell and then loosen the oyster from the bottom shell by running the oyster knife carefully underneath the body. Discard the top, flatter shell, keeping the oyster and juices in the bottom, deeper shell.

7 Put the oysters (in their bottom shells) on the grill, adding any oyster liquor from the bowl. Close the cover and cook until the juices just start to simmer and the edges of the oysters curl, 2 to 4 minutes.

8 Using tongs, transfer the oysters to the salt-lined platter. Top each oyster with some of the mignonette and parsley leaves. Drizzle with a little olive oil.

While the exact time line of the dish is unknown, lobster fra diavolo is an Italian American invention most likely born in New York's Little Italy. This preparation pares the Italian American fra diavolo sauce down to its essentials—tomatoes, garlic, and spicy red pepper flakes—and transforms it into a fresh vinaigrette perfect for pouring over briny oysters poached in their own liquor over the grill. **SERVES 4**

GRILLED OYSTERS
||| WITH ||| *fra diavolo vinaigrette*

2 tablespoons canola oil
3 garlic cloves, smashed
¼ teaspoon red pepper flakes, or more to taste
3 large very ripe beefsteak tomatoes, halved, seeded, and coarsely chopped
2 teaspoons clover honey
2 teaspoons chopped fresh oregano
3 tablespoons chopped fresh flat-leaf parsley leaves, plus more for garnish
⅓ to ½ cup extra-virgin olive oil (depending on how juicy the tomatoes are)
Kosher salt and freshly ground black pepper
20 medium to large oysters, soaked in water and scrubbed well

1 Heat the canola oil in a medium sauté pan over medium heat. Add the garlic and cook until lightly golden brown, about 2 minutes. Add the red pepper flakes and cook for 30 seconds. Add the tomatoes and cook until just heated through, about 2 minutes.

2 Transfer the mixture to a blender, add the honey, oregano, parsley, and olive oil, and blend until slightly chunky; season with salt and pepper. Transfer the vinaigrette to a bowl. (The vinaigrette can be made 1 hour ahead and kept at room temperature.)

3 Heat your grill to high for direct grilling (see page 23).

4 Evenly spread 1 cup salt on a large platter.

5 Grip each oyster, flat side up, in a folded kitchen towel. Find the small opening between the shells near the hinge and pry it open with an oyster knife. Try not to spill the delicious juices, known as the oyster liquor, in the bottom shell. Cut the oyster meat loose from the top shell and then loosen the oyster from the bottom shell by running the oyster knife carefully underneath the body. Discard the top, flatter shell, keeping the oyster and juices in the bottom, deeper shell.

6 Put the oysters (in their bottom shells) on the grill. Close the cover and cook until the juices just start to simmer and the edges of the oysters start to curl, 2 to 4 minutes.

7 Using tongs, transfer the oysters to the salt-lined platter. Top each oyster with some of the vinaigrette and chopped parsley.

Mignonette, a vinegary sauce of shallot and pepper, is a classic accompaniment to raw oysters on the half shell. It's good in its simple form, but it also stands up well to more exciting variations. This one has some kick from jalapeños, herbaceous cilantro, and fresh, tart lime juice. It's delicious served with sweet oysters that have poached in their own briny goodness atop a hot grill. **SERVES 4**

⅓ cup rice vinegar

1 tablespoon fresh lime juice

1 teaspoon clover honey

1 tablespoon finely diced red onion

1 small jalapeño, seeded and finely diced

2 tablespoons finely chopped fresh cilantro leaves

Kosher salt and freshly ground black pepper

20 oysters, soaked in water and scrubbed well

GRILLED OYSTERS
WITH *jalapeño–cilantro mignonette*

1 Heat your grill to high for direct grilling (see page 23).

2 Stir together the rice vinegar, lime juice, honey, red onion, jalapeño, and cilantro in a small bowl; season with salt and pepper. Let sit at room temperature for at least 10 minutes to allow the flavors to meld.

3 Evenly spread 1 cup salt on a large platter.

4 Grip each oyster, flat side up, in a folded kitchen towel, and work over a bowl. Find the small opening between the shells near the hinge and pry it open with an oyster knife, catching the delicious juices, known as the oyster liquor, in the bottom shell and the overflow in the bowl. Cut the oyster meat loose from the top shell and then loosen the oyster from the bottom shell by running the oyster knife carefully underneath the body. Discard the top, flatter shell, keeping the oyster and juices in the bottom, deeper shell.

5 Put the oysters (in their bottom shells) on the grill, adding any oyster liquor from the bowl. Close the cover and cook until the juices just start to simmer and the edges of the oysters start to curl, 2 to 4 minutes.

6 Using tongs, transfer the oysters to the salt-lined platter. Top each oyster with some mignonette.

MENUS

I LOVE TO ENTERTAIN OUTSIDE. *Nothing says good times better than an outdoor barbecue. Just fire up the grill and see how quickly your guests come running, cocktail in hand, all ready to jump into action and help in any way they can.* **WHILE COOKING AND EATING OUTDOORS** *is definitely more laid back than entertaining indoors, I still have a few rules, and my number one is to start with a theme. I have never understood that potluck idea where everyone brings whatever they want. I really believe that each dish has to complement the others—right down to the cocktails you serve. These are some of my favorite combinations, but, as always, feel free to get creative and create your own.*

NEW SOUTH

Smoked Trout Lettuce Wraps with Meyer Lemon Dressing and
Carrots, PAGE 225
Curry-Rubbed Smoked Chicken Thighs with Sorghum-Chile Glaze,
PAGE 124
Tomato Red Rice with Grilled Asparagus and Sweet Mint Dressing,
PAGE 107
Sparkling Bourbon Lemonade, PAGE 40

SOUTHWESTERN

Grilled Oysters with Jalapeño-Cilantro Mignonette, PAGE 274
Cold-Smoked Lamb Loin and Black Bean Tacos with Watercress
Vinaigrette, PAGE 204
Southwestern Marinated Grilled Salmon with Tomato–Red Chile
Chutney, PAGE 220
Coleslaw with Creamy Cumin-Lime-Dill Viniagrette, PAGE 78
Lime Rickey Float Margarita, PAGE 43

CARIBBEAN

Smoked Jerk Chicken Wings with Spicy Honey-Tamarind Glaze,
PAGE 118
Spicy Molasses–Rum–Glazed Rib Eyes with Jicama-Radish Salad,
PAGE 190
Grilled Corn with Spicy Brown Sugar Butter, PAGE 72
Tropical Sangria, PAGE 37

GREEK

Grilled Shrimp and Calamari with Smoked Tomato–Black Olive
Relish, PAGE 253
Lamb Patty Melts with Red Pepper–Walnut Sauce and Grilled
Onions, PAGE 210
Grilled Peppers with Feta and Dill, PAGE 90
Vodka Grape Sparkler, PAGE 38

CUBAN

Grilled Langoustines with Green Chile Mojo, PAGE 250
Cuban Skirt Steak with Tomato Escabeche and Mango Steak Sauce,
PAGE 179
Brown Sugar–Rum Grilled Sweet Potatoes with Lime Zest and
Parsley, PAGE 99
Blackberry Mojitos, PAGE 34

MEXICAN

Grilled Mushroom Escabeche Tacos, PAGE 75
Whole Red Snapper with Grilled Vera Cruz Salsa, PAGE 236
Grilled Mango with Lime, Salt, and Ancho Powder, PAGE 85
Raspberry-Peach Aqua Fresca, PAGE 39

NORTHERN ITALIAN

Grilled Shaved Asparagus Pizza with Robiola and Parsley Oil,
PAGE 63
Grilled Oysters with Crispy Pancetta–Tomato-Basil Mignonette,
PAGE 272
Fennel-Rubbed Baby Lamb Chops with Spicy Green Olive Tapanade,
PAGE 209
Lemon-Mint Prosecco Cocktail, PAGE 40

LOUISIANA

Grilled New Orleans "BBQ" Shrimp, PAGE 258
Grilled Andouille Sausage Po'boys with Spicy Aioli and Quick
Pickles, PAGE 163
Eggplant "Casserole" with Red Pepper Pesto and Cajun Bread
Crumbs, PAGE 74
Hurricane Ice Tea, PAGE 39

SPANISH

Garlic Shrimp Served on Grilled Tomato Bread, PAGE 259
Spanish Caesar Salad with Marcona Almonds and White Anchovies,
PAGE 81
Grilled Strip Steaks and Wrinkled Potatoes with Garlic Aioli and
Mojo Rojo, PAGE 182
Pisco Sour Sangria, PAGE 43

ALL-AMERICAN

Grilled Soft-Shell Crab Sandwiches with Red Slaw and Yellow
Tomatoes, PAGE 243
New Potato–Corn Chowder Salad, PAGE 91
Sweet Cherry Slushy Cups, PAGE 34

SOURCES

SPICES, DRIED CHILES, AND HOT SAUCES

www.kalustyans.com
800-352-3451

BOBBY FLAY SAUCES AND RUBS

www.bobbyflay.com

SPANISH INGREDIENTS, SUCH AS PIQUILLO PEPPERS AND SMOKED PAPRIKA

www.tienda.com
800-710-4304

SPECIALTY PRODUCE, SUCH AS FRESH CHILES

www.melissas.com
800-588-0151

CHEESES

www.murrayscheese.com
888-MY-CHEEZ (888-692-4339)

CHORIZO, LAMB, SAUSAGES, AND HOT DOGS

www.dartagnan.com
800-327-8246

FRESH LOBSTER, SEAFOOD, CHICKEN, DUCK, AND SAUSAGES

www.citarella.com
212-874-0383

BARBECUE WOOD, CHIPS, PLANKS, AND CHARCOAL

www.barbecuewood.com
800-DRYWOOD (800-379-9663)

GAS GRILLS

www.vikingrange.com
www.weber.com

CHARCOAL GRILLS, WATER SMOKERS, CHIMNEY STARTERS, GRILL GLOVES, AND GRILLING ACCESSORIES

www.weber.com
www.bbqgalore.com

CERAMIC COOKERS

www.biggreenegg.com

PIG ROASTERS, CHINA BOXES, AND LA CAJA CHINA

www.lacajachina.com
800-338-1323

ENGELBRECHT 1000 SERIES STANDARD BRATEN GRILL

www.grillsandcookers.com
866-879-3851

CUTTING BOARDS

www.boosboards.com

BOBBY FLAY GRILL PRODUCTS, PLATTERS, AND UTENSILS

www.kohls.com/bobbyflay

Note: Page references in *italics* indicate photographs.

BOBBY FLAY, a *New York Times* bestselling author, is the chef-owner of six fine-dining restaurants, including Mesa Grill, Bar Americain, and Bobby Flay Steak, and numerous Bobby's Burger Palaces. He is the host of many popular cooking shows on Food Network, from the Emmy-winning *Bobby Flay's Barbecue Addiction, Grill It! with Bobby Flay,* and *Boy Meets Grill* to the *Iron Chef America* series, *Throwdown! with Bobby Flay,* and *Food Network Star.*

STEPHANIE BANYAS has been Bobby Flay's business assistant since 1996. She is the coauthor of *Bobby Flay's Throwdown!; Bobby Flay's Burgers, Fries & Shakes; Bobby Flay's Grill It!; Bobby Flay's Mesa Grill Cookbook;* and *Bobby Flay's Grilling for Life.* She lives in New York City.

SALLY JACKSON lives in New York City with her husband, their son, and one especially well-fed poodle. This is her sixth cookbook with Bobby Flay and Stephanie Banyas.